"Get up! Get out! They are bombing!"

Julie ran from her room. Mother had taken Sammy from his bed and was holding the wailing and kicking baby. Father, his dressing gown hanging open and his feet only half lodged in old slippers, rushed to the high living-room window. He leaned out, hair askew, and pointed upwards. "Airplanes."

"What planes, Philip?"

"I—can't tell. They are not—not—ours. Oh, my God. German."

Nazi. The word drummed in Julie's mind along with the clattering aircraft that now buzzed directly overhead. Bits of paper rained down, landing on rooftops and balconies and streets. Julie pulled open the front door and dashed out into the street.

"How could you do such a thing?" Mother screamed when Julie returned with one of the leaflets. "You never listen! You run right out... what does it say? What is it?"

Father took back the paper and read slowly, in a stunned tone.... "'Germany has no hostile intent... we are here solely for the protection of the Danish people?... Do not resist....'"

"What does it mean?" Julie asked....

Mother said sharply, "We are under occupation. We are not free anymore, that's what it means."

Room in the Heart

Room in the Heart

SONIA LEVITIN

SCHOLASTIC INC.
New York Toronto London Auckland Sydney
Mexico City New Delhi Hong Kong Buenos Aires

ISBN 0-439-81074-4

12 11 10 9 8 7 6 5 4 3 7 8 9 10/0

Printed in the U.S.A. 40

First Scholastic printing, November 2005

Designed by Gloria Cheng

To *Knud Dyby*,
a real hero of our time,
with admiration and in gratitude

To *Adaire Klein*,
cherished friend, constant mentor,
lover of freedom

Acknowledgments

My sincere thanks to:

Lloyd, my husband, for always being willing to share the journey

Anne Ipsen Goldman, author of *A Child's Tapestry of War,* for her friendly and helpful correspondence

Mr. and Mrs. Erik Guttermann, of Denmark, and Rabbi Michael Jacob, of Israel, for sharing their experiences and their knowledge

Stephanie Owens Lurie, a most remarkable editor who achieves the perfect balance of mind and heart

"Where there is room in the heart,
there is room in the house."

—Danish proverb

Contents

Room IN THE Heart

Part One

APRIL 1940

CHAPTER ONE

Julie

The irritating sound circled its way into her dream—a droning, cranking noise. Julie dreamed she was atop the thatch roof of the fisherman's cabin at Humlebaek, a small child again, picking the tiny daisies that grew on the roof. A large gull came circling down, squawking and screeching.

Julie sat bolt upright. The noise seemed to come from above the rooftops, and she thought distractedly that some machine had gone awry, or perhaps a truck on the boulevard had crashed.

She ran to the window, gazing into the pearly dawn. The clock on her bookshelf said 4:35 A.M.

"Philip, for God's sake, don't just lie there, something has happened! Get up! Get up!" The screeching was her mother's voice, continuing through the rumble of Father's gruff reply.

"What is it, Edith? What?"

"Get up! Get out! They are bombing!"

Julie ran from her room. Mother had taken Sammy from his bed and was holding the wailing and kicking baby. Father, his dressing gown hanging open and his feet only half lodged in old slippers, rushed to the high living-room window. He leaned out, hair askew, and pointed upward. "Airplanes."

"What planes, Philip?"

"I—can't tell. They are not—not—ours. Oh, my God. German."

Julie's throat felt closed off. Her parents seemed to think she was unaware of the danger of Nazi invasion. As if she hadn't heard that their huge, bullying neighbor to the south had already attacked Austria, Poland, and Czechoslovakia.

Nazi. The word drummed in Julie's mind along with the clattering aircraft that now buzzed directly overhead. Suddenly the sky seemed full of shadows. Bits of paper rained down, landing on rooftops and balconies and streets.

Julie ran to the entry hall, still in semidarkness. She nearly tripped over the display case that had been knocked over by the vibration. Several canes from her father's collection lay on the floor. Julie leaped over them, pulled open the front door, and dashed out to the street. A shock of cold air accosted her.

From inside, her mother shrieked, "Julie, come back here, don't go . . ." and her father shouted, "Julie, be careful!"

Outside, the noise of the planes was terrifying, mingled with the confusion of people in nightshirts, barefoot and shouting, as they picked up the leaflets.

"How could you do such a thing?" Mother screamed when Julie returned with one of the leaflets. "You never listen! You run right out . . . what does it say? What is it?"

Julie stood in the hallway, panting and shivering.

"Father!" she shouted. "Father!" She held out the green paper.

He took the leaflet and read. "*Oprop?* What in the world does that mean?"

Mother snatched it from him, frowning. "Stupid Germans! They must mean *opraab*—'attention.' Look at this, it's full of errors, a crazy mixture of German, Danish, and Norwegian."

Father took back the paper and read slowly, in a stunned tone, "'It is Germany's sincere wish to live in peace and friendship . . . English and French people have last year declared war against Germany . . . Germany needs to act strongly against them . . . Germany has no hostile intent . . . we are here solely for the protection of the Danish people—'"

"How can that be? Our protection?" Julie broke in.

"Hush! It says it is purely precautionary. The Germans want cooperation between our countries. It says, 'Do not resist. To resist would prove disastrous to the Danish people.'"

"What does it mean?" Julie asked, impatient. "What can we do?" Sammy tugged at her nightgown. She picked him up, felt his softness against her cheek.

"Well, we don't know for certain," her father began.

Mother said sharply, "We are under occupation. We are not free anymore, that's what it means." She ran her hands through her long, dark hair. "Until they are gone from Danish soil, we cannot pretend that we are free!"

"But why are they here?" Julie cried. "How can they just come here and take over?" She clutched Sammy too tightly and he struggled, so she put him down.

"We are a stepping stone to Sweden and Norway," her father said with a heavy sigh. "They want our seaports. Hitler needs our food and materials. He takes what he wants."

"How dare he!" Julie stamped her foot. Sammy stamped, too, as if it were a game.

"Stop it!" Father caught up Sammy and moved toward the kitchen. "Edith, come, we have to eat something. Julie, we'll sit down and have a cup of tea."

Father switched on the kitchen light. It brought some feeling of life into the room, but Julie still shivered. She could not bear the thought of leaving the family circle even to go to her room for a robe. Instead, she took up the teakettle, filled it with water, and brought the tea tin from the cupboard.

As Mother prepared porridge for Sammy, Father reread the leaflet. When he spoke, his words were measured, as if he were giving a lecture. "It is most important that we learn the new rules. And there will be rules. I must talk to Cousin Boris. He understands these things, having worked for the harbor commission. Yes, I will go to him this afternoon."

Mother's eyes blazed. "I will not accept German rules!"

"We cannot resist," Father said gently, and Julie saw the pain in his eyes. "They would destroy us."

"What about our army?" Julie asked. "Why aren't we fighting?"

"Because we are terribly outnumbered," her father said. "There was probably some token resistance—the king's guard . . ." His voice trailed off uncertainly.

"Would they dare to do anything to the king?" Mother exclaimed.

Sammy banged his cup on the table. Julie went to the cooler for the milk. She watched him drink, looking up at her from the rim of his cup. A wild thought raced through her mind. *If anyone tries to hurt my brother, if they even touch a hair of Sammy's head, I will kill them!*

A common thought must have sparked between her and her mother, for Mother said, "I suppose there will be soldiers in the streets. They had better not dare to speak to me or mine. It says we must not resist. That does not mean I will offer them any comfort, not even a glance."

"Edith, Edith," Father murmured. "Please realize that you cannot control the entire nation or defeat the Nazi army. At least not in a single day or by yourself!"

Her mother laughed lightly. Julie smiled. It brought a moment of peace before the planes rumbled again, their motors sending vibrations through the house.

They ate rolls and jam and hard-boiled eggs for breakfast. Then Julie prepared their lunches of open-faced sandwiches stacked with cheese, cucumber, tomato, and small slices of pickle. Some sense of order returned. It almost seemed like a normal day, especially when Father set down his cup and said, as always, "Let's get ready, Julie. I'll ride with you and Ingrid until the crossing."

Mother asked uncertainly. "Philip, do you really think we should go out today?"

"What else can we do, Edith?"

Julie saw the struggle in her mother's face. But suddenly she sprang into action, slamming dishes into the sink, wiping up crumbs with a vigorous hand. "Yes! They are still our streets. These are still our lives. They will need me more than ever at the library. Oh, I hope Mrs. Giesler will come for Sammy. Maybe I should call her. Are the phones down? What do you think?" She turned to Father.

"She'll be here," Father said. "Everything will be fine. Just fine. I will take my bicycle on the same route as always. I will keep my eyes forward and head high. What do you say, Julie?"

Julie took a deep breath. "Head high," she repeated. But she felt a stab of annoyance at his complacency. How could he say things would be fine? She wanted—what did she want him to do? Rush out with a gun? A sword? She chided herself for being stupid and childish.

She felt her father's arm around her shoulder, warm and protective. "Come on, Julie. Help get Sammy dressed. We have to be calm. And strong."

As she buttoned Sammy into his clothes, pushed on the little shoes, once again a sense of the normal returned. The planes were gone now. Outside, all was quiet and the morning light was rising. Nothing horrible would happen, as it had in other countries, where Jews were rounded up and deported. She and her family were Danes! Oh, how Grandmother Sophie regaled the family with stories of the old days, when her great-grandparents came to Denmark and settled into the jewelry trade. "We supplied the palace with jewels, the great estates of Denmark bought our designs!" Mother's family, too, had lived in Denmark for years, long before the Russian Revolution. Nobody remembered the old languages anymore.

There is nothing to be afraid of, Julie told herself, reaching for courage.

She put on her scarf and jacket and ran out to meet her friend.

Chapter Two

Niels

That terrible racket! Niels bounded out of bed and ran to the window, knocking his shins against the low wooden table. He winced. Outside, planes roared, flying too low, sending black shadows over the streets. A few people, caught in the din, ran like frightened animals, vanishing into doorways. What could it mean? Something rained down from the sky. Bits of paper, green leaflets. They stuck to the damp streets and clung to walls. Niels stared, awestruck.

The whole household was awake now. He heard Fredericka calling their younger sister, "Ingrid! Ingrid! For God's sake, get away from that window!"

"Children!" Their mother called them together, tying her wrapper close around her body. Their father, oddly enough, was clutching the cat, that large orange-striped monster that he claimed caused him untold misery.

"Niels, see what it is," Father said in a strange voice.

Niels ran out into the predawn streets, the damp cold catching him in the chest, so that it seemed difficult to breathe. But, no, it was not the cold, for April mornings were mild compared with winter. No. It was the terrible sound of airplanes, of booted feet, of trucks with enormous black wheels rolling on the streets—*our streets,* he thought with a strange catch in his throat. He knew the German uniform, knew from newsreels and pictures the grim faces of Wehrmacht soliders.

Swiftly Niels gathered up a handful of leaflets and ran into the house. They all stood waiting for him, his father clad in gray pajamas, Mother in her blue wrapper, Fredericka, her long hair cascading around her shoulders, and Ingrid, looking pale and terrified.

Niels's father grabbed one of the leaflets and read aloud. "'People of Denmark. Do not resist. We have contracted with the Danish government . . .' We have been invaded," he declared. He looked older, as if the gray streaks in his hair had spread. He was tall and slim, and his broad shoulders, now, were slumped.

From outside came the sounds of marching feet, shouts, a crash. Niels ran to the window, drawing the lace curtain aside. Ingrid and Fredericka stood behind him; he could hear their swift breathing. They watched, stunned, as a tank made its way along the street. It seemed almost laughable, like some prehistoric gray monster come alive in the middle of Copenhagen, created just to amaze them. The long pointed gun left no illusions. Behind the tank came a squadron of motorcycles. The motorized troops roared down the street, three abreast. It almost seemed that the riders were part of their machines, their features as solid as steel.

Time felt warped, expanded. The sun was rising in the distance, and Niels saw the billowing outlines of parachutes high up in the sky.

Everyone gathered around the radio. Father lifted his hand for silence and moved closer as the words snapped out from amid static. ". . . urged to proceed in a normal manner to your places of work, children to school, government workers to their offices. It is vital that we keep calm. King Christian has agreed that our government and the Danish citizens will give full cooperation to the German Wehrmacht. We must stand together in our resolve. God bless Denmark! God bless the king!"

The national anthem began playing. The music surged into the room. "There is a lovely land . . ." Ingrid sang in a soft, childish voice. Fredericka took up the song, and then Mother joined them. Father stood by, remote and silent. Niels looked down, oddly embarrassed, yet moved. A sound escaped from his throat, unwittingly. He put his hand over his mouth.

When it was over, Fredericka lashed out at Niels. "What are you laughing about, Niels? This is serious—have you no sense and no feelings?"

"Who's laughing?" he retorted. "Why do you always start—"

"That's enough!" said their father. "At least let us have peace in the house."

"He is mocking us!" Fredericka cried.

Mother stepped between them. "Hush! We are all nervous and shaken. Now get dressed, children. We will do exactly what the king wishes. We will mind our business and get on with our day. Fredericka, I want you to take the bus with me."

"But, Mor—"

A look silenced Fredericka. Today there would be no argument about girlfriends and not wanting to be seen with one's mother, a chemistry teacher, when one was in the last year of *gymnasium,* after all, and ought not to be treated like a child!

Suddenly Mother again assumed her position as general. That was what Father often called her, teasing, "Ask the general, don't ask me. I only live here!"

No jokes today, only orders. "Ingrid, get dressed."

"I *am* dressed, Mor!" Ingrid objected. She was the only one who had leaped into her clothes at the first sign of trouble. Probably some lesson in school had given warning: in emergency, be prepared.

"What about school?" Niels asked. "Do we have to go?"

"Yes, you must. First eat something, Niels. Ingrid, I want you to wait inside until you see Julie and Mr. Weinstein, then stay with them. Stay close. Do whatever Mr. Weinstein tells you."

"Mor, you treat me like a baby!"

Niels pulled her aside. "Come on," he said. "Let's slice some bread. We'll make tea for Far, coffee for us." Ordinarily they were not allowed coffee, except a mere taste in hot milk. Today was different.

Out in the kitchen Niels and Ingrid hastily set out breakfast—sliced dark bread, jam, some leftover herring salad, and coffee. He rushed to his room, dressed quickly, and made his bed. When he returned to the kitchen it was empty. Usually Mother would be making lunches, Father reading the paper, and the girls squabbling about something or other. The teakettle bubbled and hissed. Niels turned off the flame.

Fredericka came in, looking as if she had been crying. Today, nobody sat down. Father drank his tea leaning against the counter, his eyes over the cup looking very deep set, very tired.

Mother joined them a few minutes later, dressed in a dark blue print dress and the black boots she usually wore for school. Her fair hair was pinned on top of her head, and she wore the same jewelry as always, a silver brooch at her collar and small pearl stud earrings. She took a cup of tea and a slice of dry bread. She alone sat down at the table, spread the bread with jam, cut it into four pieces, and sat staring at it.

"Niels," she said, "will you be going with Emil?"

"Yes, Mor," he replied.

She looked at Fredericka and Ingrid, drinking coffee. She seemed about to object, but she only sighed and turned to Father. "Will you be at the hospital later?"

"Of course, Kirsten." They exchanged a long look.

"Tonight we have to—I want to talk."

"I'm going now," Niels said. The din from outside had subsided to a low rumble of trucks and marching feet. It seemed a matter of honor to go, not to hide indoors. "I'll eat at Emil's house."

His father stopped him. "Niels, keep a cool head. Don't do anything to provoke—"

"I won't, Far, I promise. But please, let me go."

"Let him go, Karl," his mother said quietly. "Fredericka, you have sewing club this afternoon." She stood up, in charge again, the lines about her mouth very deep and firm. "Ingrid, I expect you will go to Julia's house after school for your piano lesson."

Ingrid's mouth fell open. "I—I . . ."

"I am sure your teacher will be there. As always."

Niels saw sudden tears in Ingrid's eyes. "Is this a war?" Her voice quaked. "Are we in it?"

"I suppose you could say we are half in," said Mother, "and half out." She took a deep breath. "We have some guests in our land. They were not invited, but we are civilized people. We don't like trouble."

"Are we cowards, then?" Niels asked boldly.

"Never say such a thing again!" Mother cried. "Do you call King Christian a coward? It is not so simple, this matter of war or peace. As for you, keep your mouth shut and go about your own business, and let me hear no more talk of cowards!"

Niels took his knapsack and jacket and went outside. People gathered together, muttering, their faces stern as they tried to sort out the assault on their senses. Soldiers and trucks, tanks and rifles—it was alarming, but they refused to show any alarm.

Control, Niels thought, that is our strength.

He opened the narrow gate and took his bicycle out of the shed that dominated the small yard. He turned and saw Ingrid at the doorway. In her school skirt and sweater she looked gangly, with those long legs of hers and typical thirteen-year-old awkwardness. She had a way of hugging her arms to her chest, as if to deny any feminine development. On the other hand, she and Julie fussed with their hair and clothes for hours. He knew for a fact they had spent an entire day buying brassieres, because they had whispered and giggled about it all that night. It was hard to understand girls, Niels thought, though he should have had plenty of practice. Fredericka, imagining herself an adult at sixteen, continually instructed him, as if he were a child, and not just a year younger.

Niels swung onto his bike and pedaled quickly, unbuttoning his jacket as he rode. Sometimes in April an icy wind still blew from the north, but today it was mild, with sunshine flickering through the budding trees.

A green army truck now rode beside him, filled with soldiers. All had rifles. The truck sped up, then stopped. The soldiers jumped out. Several of them pulled bicycles from the truck. Others marched in pairs up the street, swaggering as if they owned the city.

Niels did not look back, though he wanted to. He would pretend they did not exist.

He heard a loud pounding. Probably a boot against a bolted door. He heard a shout. *"Auf machen!"* He knew the German words, "Open up!" for his major in school was modern languages. Ironically he wondered, was this the purpose of his studies? To be able to respond to the conquerors? He sped up, pedaling fast, trying to dispel these odd thoughts.

He passed other cyclists now, and pedestrians. And he felt a sense of kinship, a sudden love that reached across all boundaries. They were all Danes, together in this moment of trial, Danes and proud of it.

Chapter Three

Julie

Father always rode with them to the bridge. Then they parted. He called it his "morning constitutional," before he made his way downtown to the jewelry store, an old, elegant place, established on Bredgade Street for some two hundred years. Julie pressed her fingers together, feeling the silver ring on her right hand. She and Ingrid had gotten matching rings when they were twelve. Of course, her father had arranged it with the designer—interlocking circles with a small star sapphire in the center.

She caught sight of Ingrid, waiting, leaped from her bicycle, and let it lie on the curb. "Ingrid! Oh, I'm so glad to see you!"

"Wasn't it awful?" Ingrid exclaimed. "Have you seen the tanks? The soldiers?"

"Of course," Julie said. "We saw everything from down the street. Come on, Far's in a lather. We have to hurry, he says."

Her father waved to Ingrid and called, "Good morning! Come along, we'll take the usual route. Look straight, girls," he called almost gaily as they rode past five or six green-clad soldiers. The soldiers carried rifles. Their faces gave no clue that they were strangers in a strange place.

Julie and Ingrid rode side by side. Julie kept her eyes on her father's cap of dark blue wool, an artist's beret. It was a bit embarrassing. Nobody else she knew wore a beret. Her heart pounded, as if she had been racing, hard.

They rode past the bakery. The fragrance of fresh bread and rolls wafted out to the street. Julie heard a loud slamming sound and turned in time to see several soldiers, their arms loaded with bread and cakes, leaving the shop. One gave a mighty backward kick at the bakery door. Julie's heart lurched. The proprietress, Bente Jensen, was the sort to lean over the counter, providing little children with extra cookies. Julie had known her since she was a baby. The thought of German soldiers confronting Bente Jensen, maybe stealing her wares, made Julie furious. She slowed, imagining herself stepping inside the bakery, shrieking at the soldiers, "How dare you!"

"Come, girls. See nothing," intoned Mr. Weinstein.

"Three monkeys," Julie muttered. *Hear no evil, see and speak no evil—but how can we stand it?*

They were almost at the bridge, after which the school was only four blocks away. Julie's face felt hot, her legs ached. Her father paused, as if he meant to go with them to the middle school. But Julie waved him on. "We're fine," she called, with a good deal more confidence than she felt. "Go on, Far! We'll be fine."

Her father waved, and Julie watched him ride away. She and Ingrid rode on to the school. But they stopped in horror as they saw that the school had been invaded. Swarms of soldiers, some with motorbikes, others pouring from trucks, crowded the sidewalk, the lawn, and the porch, barring the main door.

At the sides of the building, teachers were stationed, waving their arms, calling out, "Students, you must enter from the side doors."

"They are using the school grounds to regroup," snapped out the principal, a stern man, now flushed and ramrod straight. "They will be gone soon. Girls, go to your classes. Go to your classes!" He pointed, like a traffic policeman.

Students were pushing, their faces tense, crowding into the doorways.

"Maybe we should go home," Julie said as they left their bicycles in the rack.

"Maybe not—they are telling us to go in."

"Students—inside the building, hurry!" the principal called.

"What if they decide to take over the school? What if they won't leave?" Ingrid said. "How can we just pretend they aren't here?"

Julie thought of Helga, her young piano teacher, and how she had once told Julie, "We pretended a lot in Berlin, maybe too much. We Jews are good pretenders."

Wordless, Julie and Ingrid walked together into the building.

Julie felt Ingrid close beside her. Their hands touched. "Are you scared?" Julie whispered.

"No," Ingrid whispered back.

"Neither am I," Julie lied.

They entered the classroom. Two German soldiers stood at the head of the class, flanking the teacher's desk. Everyone sat down quickly, without noise. The presence of the soldiers made the room seem small and irrelevant. They were from another world—the world of noise and steel and menace.

"Be seated quickly and quietly, children," said the teacher. She was tall and thin, dressed as usual in a gray pencil slim skirt and matching blouse. Julie couldn't even guess her age—somewhere between twenty-five and forty-five, she supposed. But the teacher now looked frail. Her hands, folded in front of her, twitched and clutched, and she moistened her lips too often. "These gentlemen," she said with a strange inflection, a slight cough, "have come to tell us about the new order in Denmark. Let us pay close attention, girls."

Julie sat stiffly in her seat, hands flat on her desk. She felt the presence of Ingrid and the others, all of them stunned and mute. *A new order.* The words sounded dreadful, un-Danish.

"We are coming here as your friends," the soldier said. "Friends must treat each other with respect . . ."

Julie turned her head slightly to look at Ingrid. Ingrid's hand was at her chin, so that the star sapphire glowed, like a signal between them.

The soldier gave the class a condescending look. He was the victor, the ruler, deigning to address them. His words were an odd mixture of Danish and German, and the students might have laughed, except that they had been taught courtesy—and then there was the matter of the pistol at his side. He attempted a smile.

Suddenly Julie remembered a terrible poster she had seen months ago, at the Jewish Community library, where her mother worked. She and Father had stopped in for some errand. While she waited, Julie had wandered to a shelf filled with pamphlets and papers, one labeled NAZI PROPAGANDA. A poster showed photographs of children in two columns, one side titled ARYAN, the other JEWS. The Aryan children were blond, blue-eyed, well formed, and strong. Their counterparts were dark and ugly, with huge noses and leering eyes. Beneath the pictures were the words, in Danish, "Let us keep our racial purity. Expel the hateful Jews!"

She had still been reading the literature, trembling, when her father returned and asked what was the matter. "What is this? What does it mean?" she had cried out.

"Oh, just some nonsense. It has nothing to do with us, Julie. Come, let's go."

Now, as the soldier spoke, Julie cast her glance around the room. She met Ingrid's eyes. Ingrid, with her high cheekbones, blue eyes, and blond hair, was the Nazi's ideal. Her whole life Julie had lived the principles that nobody seemed to doubt: we are all free, all equal, all Danes. Now, for the first time, she felt conspicuously different, with her curly dark hair, brown eyes, and deep complexion. She was one of the shortest girls in the class. The Nazi, gazing out at the students, had probably already spotted her as an alien. They made these distinctions. They labeled people, classified them, as in that horrible poster.

Julie remembered asking Helga, when they first met, why she had left Germany. Helga had tensed visibly, picking at her cuticle and sucking in her lip. "Well, the Nazis were making terrible laws, you know. I was not allowed to attend public school anymore. My father—he published a small Jewish newspaper. They came and smashed his printing press. It got so bad, Julie, they wanted me to get out to safety."

"But why didn't your parents come with you?"

"They will join me later," Helga had said, "in Palestine. Look, it is complicated, but I am sure everything will be fine. We must be happy, Julie! Let me hear you play the Chopin. Our recital is next month, and you must have a happy heart to play well!"

Now the soldier droned on, saying, "Nothing need change for you here. We Germans are big brothers to the Danes. Don't you think we will take care of our little brothers?"

Julie caught Ingrid's eye and exchanged the merest signal.

Later she and Ingrid would imitate the Nazi's stance and his accent. They would make a play, a mockery, of the moment.

They shared everything—even piano, which Ingrid had no flair for, but she practiced at Julie's house, and they shared Helga, the teacher.

Helga, at twenty, was more like an older friend than a teacher. She adored Copenhagen, and the three went often to see the sights, the harbors with the huge ships and small pleasure craft, the beautiful parks filled with lilies and tulips in the spring. Helga especially loved Tivoli Gardens, and the late afternoon concerts. Sometimes there were mimes. Helga would watch them, entranced, clapping her hands. "Be happy, children," she would say, laughing, including herself in the admonishment. "It takes courage to be happy."

Now Julie she kept her eyes downcast. To look at the Nazi meant acknowledgment, almost acceptance. She refused to even to think of it, instead forced herself to breathe deeply and think good thoughts. *Be happy.*

Chapter Four

Niels

As Niels rode toward Emil's house, he recalled the war games they used to play, leaping into ditches, climbing trees, chasing, shouting, pretending that their sticks were rifles, *Bam! Bam!*

The reality, he thought, is always different from the game. He wanted more than anything to talk to Emil, to share his outrage and to hear Emil's lusty plans. Always a person of action, Emil would have ideas about what to do, where to go, how to behave.

Unbelievable! Germany and Denmark had signed a nonaggression pact only a year ago. Every schoolboy knew about it. It meant that the two nations would never make war or launch an invasion against each other. Well, they simply did not call it an invasion, Niels thought, filled with scorn. Call it something else—*occupation*—and it is all right!

Several sleek, black cars rolled past him, slowly, as if showing off their insignia, lording it over cyclists and pedestrians. Even the automobiles, with their German Volkswagen emblems, were an affront.

Niels thought of his father's rusty old Opel, a necessity, for he spent many nights at the distant Bispebjerg Hospital checking on his patients after surgery. Niels wondered, would his father still go out on rounds at night, with the tanks and soldiers on the streets? His father was a mild and peaceful man. This morning, when the planes came and dropped their vicious cargo, his father's face had turned white, and his hands, usually so steady, had trembled.

It was painful to admit it even to himself; he did not know his father well. There had always been this distance, his father preoccupied with thoughts of the hospital and doctoring. There was a too-clean smell about him, something artificial. His father cared little for sailing. He was downright inept with motors and fishing gear. Nor did he bicycle, even for pleasure. Strange, Niels thought, how his father could enjoy being indoors all day. Surely there were doctors who also loved to smell the sea air.

Niels hurried past the park, riding along the rise from which he could see the harbor clearly. Just so, from the other side of the quay, the German boats must have entered, releasing their soldiers from within, like a Trojan horse landing under the cover of darkness.

Emil's street was the one with a row of houses painted bright yellow, with a peaked brown roof. Each windowsill was decorated with urns and flowerpots, candlesticks and ornaments of pewter and bronze. For a moment Niels imagined it all gone, swept away in a flash of smoke and fire. He took a deep breath and groaned as he realized surrender had been the only reasonable choice. "We are weak," he murmured. "Weak and small." It left a queasy feeling in his stomach, so that when he got to Emil's door, his friend's mother pulled him inside anxiously.

"Are you all right, Niels? You look as if you have seen a ghost. But of course, we are all half mad from fright and shock. Except for Emil. He is rummaging up in the attic, as usual. Can you imagine?"

In the background the radio sounded its constant, sharp announcements: ". . . urged to remain calm. Danish police will cooperate with German forces. Danish police will detain and punish anyone engaged in lawless activities or sabotage."

His thoughts flew to his uncle Jens, a policeman. On sunny afternoons he and Jens often met at Ny Haven to sit at one of the small tables or on the seawall. Girls slowed their steps and smiled when they saw Jens.

Niels was neither tall nor pale blond, like Jens and like Emil. Solid, his mother called him. With that word Niels imagined a tree, not a handsome knight or royal guardsman. Jens, in fact, had served for a year as a royal guard, and everyone knew these men were chosen at least in part for their good looks.

Niels climbed the stairs to the upper floor, where a narrow wooden ladder hung down from the attic opening. He called, "Emil! Come down—what are you doing?"

"Getting things," came the answer, amid puffing and gasping and the sounds of boxes being moved. "For the boat."

"Are you crazy? Do you think now we just go sailing anytime we want?"

Emil poked his head down through the opening. His full, round face was red from exertion, and his pale blond hair stood straight up. He grinned at Niels and countered, "Do you think that anyone can keep me out of the sea?"

Niels chuckled. "I suppose not."

Emil's mother came halfway up the stairs, calling, "Breakfast! Niels, you will eat with us." It was a statement, not a question.

"Yes, thank you, Mor." He had always called Emil's mother Mor, just like his own mother. The family friendship went all the way back to their grandfathers, who went to sea together, fishing for herring and later taking excursions of tourists across the sound to Sweden.

They went down to the small dining room, where Emil's mother was bustling about nervously. "I'm afraid I have not prepared much," she apologized. "Only coffee and rolls and cheese. What a terrible morning! Gustav ran out to see to the boats—he was only worried about his boats. Left me here to face God knows what . . ."

"Well, you had me to look after you, Mor," said Emil. "Anyhow, those Germans won't bother us. You heard it yourself. They have come here only to protect themselves against a possible invasion."

"Who would want to invade Germany?" Niels asked, astonished.

"Anyone—the French, the British. It is war, after all."

"But the Germans started it!" Niels cried.

Emil spread his roll thickly with butter and cheese. "Look, as long as they leave us alone . . ."

From the radio came the steady stream of information, assurance, warnings: ". . . to stay away from military installations. The harbor, as well as the Citadel, has been taken by German forces . . ."

Niels saw an expression of sudden interest leap into his friend's face.

Emil got up abruptly, stuffing several rolls into his knapsack. "We have to go, Mor. Take a roll with you, Niels. We'll be late, and we have examinations today, don't your remember?"

Niels started to speak, saw the warning glint in Emil's eyes. "Yes, yes," he said. "Of course. Exams." Emil thrust a roll into his hand and pulled him outdoors. "Let's leave our bikes. We'll run to school. I want to run."

"Good-bye, Mor Hansen," Niels called back. "Thank you."

"Careful, careful," she warned from the doorway, waving.

Once past the house, Emil broke into a run. Niels followed, panting, "What's that about exams? And where are we going?"

"To the harbor. I want to see."

"Are you crazy? That's where the Germans are—they came in on ships. They have taken the Citadel . . ."

"I know it!" Emil turned around, his feet still tapping with impatience. "What's the matter with you, Niels? Don't you want to see for yourself? Are you like the old ones, just sitting and biting their nails? Come on!"

"What about school?"

"What about it? Nobody expects us to go today. Nobody will question us—if they do, we will say my father needed us to help secure the boats against the Germans. We'll think of something. Come on!"

They ran behind the Citadel, approaching from the side, behind the old church where prisoners used to pray and the militia held their Sunday service. Elm trees were just barely coming into bloom. The grass was crisp and green from winter rains. Groups of soldiers marched below them, forming squadrons, guarding the doors of the offices. The boys could hear the sounds of their boots and the loud, guttural shouts of commanders. Men rushed into position. The Nazi salute was swift and harsh, the gesture of a swordsman.

Niels and Emil walked slowly, cautiously, down toward the gate where three soldiers stood guard.

Emil put his arm across Niels's chest. "Move slowly," he warned, "and don't say anything. Or do you want to practice your German?"

Niels's mouth felt dry. His German was fairly good, but to speak to these men seemed somehow unpatriotic.

Slowly the boys drew closer to the three soldiers. They wore the brownish green uniforms and helmets, with straps that cut into their throats. Their expressions were tense, eyes straight ahead, their features like granite. All had rifles, one on his shoulder, the other two thrust forward, at the ready.

"Halt!" one solider shouted, stepping forward with a smart click of his heels.

Niels's heart pounded with fear and excitement. He had never felt this way, not even when the waves rose high, nearly capsizing the boat he and Emil were sailing. There was something compelling and urgent about danger coming close enough to touch and taste.

"Raus!" The soldier gestured unmistakably with his rifle, meaning, "Get out of here." *"Was wollenn Sie hier?"*

Emil murmured to Niels, "What's he saying?"

"We're supposed to leave."

Emil nodded calmly, hands in his pockets. "We just wanted to look at you," he said slowly, in Danish.

"Verboten, Sie können nicht . . ."

Two of the soldiers muttered together, their faces still taut. The third stepped forward and said in broken Danish, "It is not allowed to be here. Must you leave. I am sorry."

Another of the soldiers shouted out, *"Verschwindet! Oder, wollen Sie eine blaue Bohne?"*

The others laughed, a loud, raucous sound. Niels felt frozen to the spot. He caught the gaze of one of the soldiers, who now lit a cigarette. Niels smelled the smoke from the cigarette and saw the firm lines of the soldier's jaw. Their gazes met. Niels felt the shock of that moment's meeting, thinking, He's so young! Just a few years older than we. Would he kill? It seemed impossible that a man, hardly more than a boy, could actually be capable of killing.

"See, they are human beings," Emil said, "just like us. And they are well trained," he added with undisguised admiration. "Come on, let's go to school now. I have seen enough."

Niels felt the pavement altered beneath him, the very air tainted, foreign and bitter.

"What was he saying there, at the end?" Emil asked.

"He said, 'Get out of here. Or do you want a blue bean?'"

"A blue bean?"

"German slang," said Niels. "It means a bullet."

CHAPTER FIVE

Julie

"Only fourteen people," Julie's mother complained as she battled the large cooking pots, preparing chickens, fish, soup, and countless side dishes.

"Isn't fourteen people enough, Edith?" Father moved swiftly through his woman's domain, standing aside from the flurry. "You tire yourself needlessly."

"We always have twenty or more at the Seder," Mother said, wiping a bit of steam from her face with her apron. On the stove before her, the chicken soup bubbled gently. She went on, "Bella's boy will ask the Four Questions."

"Of course. He's the youngest," Father said. "Why is that boy always yelling?"

"Maybe because nobody listens to him," replied Mother.

Julie remembered being the youngest child, entrusted with that special task of asking, "Why is this night different from all other nights?" to begin the Passover story.

Tonight nine-year-old Sasha would recite the Four Questions, and Julie could just imagine Aunt Bella fussing around him all day. Bella and Aleksander were the "frum" part of the family. They belonged to the Orthodox synagogue and meticulously kept the Sabbath restrictions against driving or lighting lamps or even using the telephone.

"Did Bella check the menu with you?" Father asked, half joking.

"No need," replied mother tartly. "She knows I would only serve kosher meat. Don't worry, Philip. I know what is correct." Mother continued her litany. "Aunt Monica is not up to coming here. She hardly leaves her room at the Home."

"Don't they have a Seder there?" Julie asked. She had been working with her mother all morning, chopping apples, peeling potatoes, mixing dough.

"Of course they have a Seder," Mother said briskly. "But it isn't the same. I'll miss her, the dear."

Father moved nearer, placing his hands on Mother's shoulders. "Don't worry. Tonight will be wonderful."

"I'm *not* worrying! You miss the point, Philip. On a holiday, one does not want an empty table with empty chairs. Everyone should be together."

Father shot Julie a grin. He shrugged helplessly. Julie laughed and said, "Mother invited four extra people to take up the chairs. Fredericka, Ingrid, Helga, and a student—what do you call him?"

"Halutz," said mother. "It means 'pioneer.' He came here to study farming before settling in Palestine. Now he is stuck here."

At quarter to five, when the doorbell rang, Julie ran to answer it, expecting Ingrid and Fredericka. Instead, there stood a young man, about eighteen, with dark hair down to the nape of his neck, and intense, friendly brown eyes. He wore a brown tweed coat in a style and fabric Julie had never seen before. And he was handsome, with a firm jaw and wide mouth, breaking into a smile. A flush came to Julie's cheeks. She was glad for her new dress, a two-piece maroon velvet with buttons of real onyx and a narrow black leather belt. Her shoes were brand-new, too, black leather with antique silver buckles.

"Hello," she said, smiling broadly. "Come in! You must be the *halutz* student."

He extended his hand, and she took it, feeling the strong warmth. "I am Peter Peretsky," he said. "Your mother was kind enough to invite me. I took the train. Hope I am not too early, but the train schedule is sometimes unreliable."

"Shall I take your coat?"

"No, thank you. It was a cold walk from the station." He stood in the entry, rubbing his hands together, eyeing the display case with its velvet backing and several canes. "Someone here must be a collector," he said. Peter smiled, and his eyes shone. "Your father?"

"Yes. How can you tell?" She laughed. "He loves those canes, spends hours reading catalogs, writing letters, and studying histories."

"I can imagine," Peter said. "My father collected bottle stoppers, all sorts. He kept them on special shelves under glass." He moved toward the case, looking closely. "These are beauties."

"Yes, yes indeed." Julie tried to infuse her tone with genuine appreciation; the canes were simply a part of her existence, nothing remarkable. She wished now for some knowledge or enthusiasm she could impart to Peter. In the American movies she and Ingrid saw, the girls were always ready with quick remarks. She and Ingrid and Fredericka would argue over the leading men. Julie loved Tyrone Power the best; his dark good looks thrilled her, and he was dashing and brave. Ingrid's favorite was Gary Cooper, the tall, slim, drawling American. She loved cowbo

Now all Julie's fantasies were replaced by this reality, Peter Peretsky, handsome and smart, and she could think of nothing to say. She felt the beat of her own heart in her throat. In the movies the women knew just how to be amusing or provocative.

"Come, come into the living room," Julie said. "There is a fire." They would sit down and talk together. Her mind raced over some possible topic. Bottle stoppers? Canes? Maybe farming—but what did she know about cows? "Do you like movies?" she asked.

"Of course. But we don't see many on the farm." He laughed.

Stupid! she thought with a pang of misery. He must think I'm an idiot. He's so handsome! So nice! I must be crazy. What is wrong with me? I wish . . .

A new thought interrupted her reverie. He would be perfect for Helga. Yes, poor Helga, all alone in Denmark. Now she would have someone, a boyfriend. It was perfect.

◆ ◆ ◆

Aunt Bella brought an overabundance of flowers, enough for every table in the house. She carried in huge bunches of tulips and daylilies, white asters and lavender, calling out, "Edith, oh, Edith! I hope you have plenty of vases. Sasha, take off your jacket—get away from the piano. Edith, isn't it terribly hot in here? The flowers will be absolutely destroyed."

Julie introduced her to Peter as "my aunt Bella," though she was not really an aunt at all, but a second or third cousin on Mother's side, a part of the family that had come from Lithuania years ago. All families, Julie supposed, had this confused ta[illegible] of aunts, uncles, and cousins, real or honorary. There was [illegible] another distant cousin, and his son, Michael, a young [illegible]y. Whatever had happened to the rest of their family

Julie did not know. Michael and the old man were always together, always in an argument. It began with the seating, when Boris motioned Michael away from the head of the table. "You think you are the boss here? That place is for the older generation."

Michael grunted, shook his head, and shuffled to the other side of the table, beside Aleksander. He whispered to Aleksander, casting baleful glances at his father, who patted his pockets, searching for a forbidden cigar. Aleksander sat in his usual posture, leaning on one elbow, fingers scrambling through his beard, a dark, uneven mass.

It was like every Seder, the fine table linen, the good silver, the gleaming bottles of wine, with Father leading prayers, telling the ancient story. "Because we were slaves in Egypt, do we now celebrate our freedom . . . on that watch night, when angry crowds came to pursue us . . . we pray for the freedom of all people . . ."

Sasha, wearing a bright, embroidered *kippa,* shouted out the Four Questions in Hebrew: "Why is this night different from all other nights . . . ?" His parents beamed their approval. When he was finished, everyone clapped, and Sammy shrieked loudly.

"Soon Sammy will be asking the questions."

"Ah, how time flies. I remember when it was Julie."

"And before that, our Rina. Remember, Aleksander, how nervous she was?"

It all seemed like a scene from a play, familiar and practiced. But tonight there was also a different atmosphere. Was it her imagination, or was everyone struggling to restrain the conversation, as if certain words, once spoken, would bring disaster crashing down upon them?

After the service came dinner, huge platters and bow'

brimming full. There were the rousing compliments, echoing through the room, and Julie's mother smiled and protested and smiled all the more.

"Ah, these are the best matzo balls I have ever eaten, Edith! Do you add onions?"

"Look at that roast—you could cut it with a fork."

"The chicken is absolutely fabulous."

"Come, let us drink *l'chaim*—to life!"

Julie looked around the table. She wanted to memorize the moment, the faces of family and friends. Sammy had fallen asleep, leaning sideways in his high chair. Fredericka gently picked him up and held him on her lap.

Grandmother Sophie smiled warmly at Julie. "Are you doing well in school, darling?"

"Yes, Grandmother."

"She is second in her class, Mama," Mother put in.

"And who is first?" Grandmother asked, chuckling. "Never mind, darling. You have many accomplishments. Are you taking up tennis? When I was your age, I played nearly every day."

She began talking with Uncle Aleksander and Aunt Bella. "Yes, surely we will go to the coast this summer, but after the yacht races. I have never missed them, not in forty years." Dressed in a beautiful black cashmere dress with lace collar and cuffs, Grandmother Sophie looked like a queen, Julie thought. Several large rings gleamed as she gestured. Her hair, steel gray, was full and fashionably swept up in front.

Helga sat beside Peter Peretsky. Julie heard bits of their conversation, about Mozart and some festival. She wished she could of something to say to Peter, but simply watching him ough to make her feel flushed and extraordinarily happy. e was animated; his laughter brightened the room. He glanced at Fredericka time after time. It felt as if a circle were drawn around Peter Peretsky, with everyone surrounding him, admiring him.

"It is a very nice farm, with produce and livestock," Peter said, in reply to Father's question. "We are learning how to raise chickens and to make cheese. It will be a very important industry in Palestine."

"Oh, you are going to Palestine!" Helga exclaimed. "How wonderful. Will you be living on a kibbutz?"

"I hope so," Peter replied. "Of course, now everything is up in the air. We are just biding our time, waiting. The Germans won't let us leave."

"It was also my hope to go there," Helga said softly.

"You are from Germany, my dear?" Grandmother asked, leaning toward Helga.

"Yes, ma'am. My parents sent me here with the Youth Aliyah children."

"Some of them have already gone to Palestine," Peter put in. "Now, if we could somehow get a permit . . ." He frowned deeply.

"You need a permit for everything," Boris grumbled loudly. "Permit to travel, even to go to the bathroom—pardon me. Damned bureaucrats!"

"Father, there is nothing to get excited about," Michael protested. "No wonder your blood pressure goes up and up."

"I know what it is to live under dictatorship," Boris cried. "Believe me, in Russia we were persecuted under the czar, always in danger of being conscripted. I have been here for thirty-five years, and you may be shocked when I tell you, my passport is always in order. I am ready to run."

"Now, Father," said Michael, "that's absurd. Everyone knows that Denmark is different." He turned away, exasperated.

"Don't worry, Boris," said Uncle Aleksander. "The Germans will not start any trouble here. They know the Danes oppose any action against Jews—or any group, for that matter."

Aunt Bella pointed meaningfully. Aleksander brushed several offending crumbs from his beard with a napkin.

"Ya, ya, they know," said Boris, taking a cigar from his pocket, quickly putting it away as both Bella and Mother frowned. "Well, I have my old navy cap, and I mean to wear it, and also my lapel pin." He showed the pin, an enamel insignia of the king. There was silence.

Michael addressed himself to Peter. "How do you like Copenhagen?"

"I have not seen much of it," Peter replied. "Only the harbor, when I arrived. We were taken immediately to the farm, and I have been working there ever since."

"You mean you have not been to Tivoli?" Fredericka exclaimed.

"Perhaps you and your friends would show it to me," said Peter. "I will be staying in Copenhagen for a few days. It would be a kindness."

"We would be happy to do that," said Fredericka boldly, meeting Peter's gaze.

Grandmother Sophie wiped her glasses and placed them neatly in her jeweled case. "And where do you stem from, Mr. Peretsky?" she asked formally.

"Czechoslovakia, ma'am. I was lucky to have left before the Nazis marched in and took over the country. My parents are [illegible]onists. They're hoping to meet me in Palestine."

[illegible]a's voice rang out. "What is a Zionist?"

[illegible]n't yell, Sasha!" snapped his mother. "What is the matter [illegible]?"

"Somone who wants a homeland for the Jewish people, a country to call their own," Uncle Aleksander said.

"Why would they want a whole country of their own?"

The adults looked at one another ruefully.

"Because they are persecuted in nearly every land!" answered Michael.

"Psst!" shot out Boris. "Leave the boy his innocence!"

Grandmother turned to Helga. "And your parents? Will they go to Palestine, too?"

Helga bit her lip, her eyes downcast. "That was the plan, ma'am. My parents sent me out first because . . ."—she took a deep breath—"because things were getting unpleasant for us in Germany. We had no idea how the evil would grow."

Everyone's eyes were upon Helga now. Julie scarcely dared to breathe. Beside her Ingrid, too, sat motionless.

"My parents wanted me to go on with my education in Denmark. They would follow, they said. But on Kristallnacht my father was . . ." Helga picked up her wineglass. Julie saw how Helga's hand trembled as she set the glass down again, without drinking. "You know how the Nazis went out that night, looting stores, burning down synagogues. The fire brigade watched them burn. They did nothing! Mama wrote me a letter afterward. The telephone lines were down. I did not know for days what had happened."

Julie listened, unable to take her eyes from Helga's face, from those trembling lips. She wanted to cover her ears and shout for Helga to stop! Disaster seemed certain, creeping into this very room.

"The Nazis—they filled the streets, shouting and smashing things. They dragged my father out of the apartment, where h
was sleeping, above the print shop. He had just begun to reb

to publish again. They dragged him out and beat him right there on the street. Beat him to death." Helga's voice broke.

"Oh, my soul!" Grandmother gasped. The room seemed bound in a terrible mist, cold and contaminating. Julie could not look at anyone. Passover. Seder. It meant order, ritual, family and friends together in gratitude for freedom. Now it seemed like a sham.

"My dear, dear child," whispered Bella. She reached out for Sasha, who was standing beside her, and drew him close.

"What a terrible thing," Julie's mother said. "Is there anything we can do for your mother?"

Helga shook her head. She stood up. "You must excuse me," she said. "I promised my landlady I'd be home by ten. She wants to lock up personally after I am in."

"Will you be all right?" Father asked. "Shall someone walk with you?"

"I have my bicycle," Helga said. "Please, do not interrupt the evening."

Michael rose to his feet. "Please, let me accompany you."

Helga hesitated, then nodded. "Very well. Thank you."

But it was impossible to return to the celebration. Mother brought out the Passover sponge cake and macaroons and tall glasses of hot tea. Grandmother sipped her tea, sighing, dabbing at her eyes. "That poor, dear girl." She sighed.

"And where is her mother now?" Bella wondered. "Probably stuck in Berlin, maybe even deported to a concentration camp. Who knows? We hear such dreadful things."

haps she can get out to Switzerland or someplace safe," said. She exchanged a glance with Father, then turned to nd Julie. "I'm sorry you girls had to hear this. But on the other hand, you would learn these things eventually. We cannot hide the truth any longer."

"Edith," Father said softly, "it is Passover. We must be thankful for our own freedom now, especially now."

The candles flickered. Darkness seemed to crowd the room, held in by the blackout curtains. Julie looked at Ingrid and saw tears in her friend's eyes. She wished time could stop, keep them safe all together.

"You know what?" Father said. "We forgot the song 'An Only Kid.' We will do it now. All together!"

Wavering at first, they sang, with Sasha's voice leading and everyone joining in. When they called out, "Next year in Jerusalem!" Julie glanced at Peter, who raised his glass and called out, "Amen!"

Chapter Six

Fredericka's Diary

All night at the Seder, I thought it was Helga he was interested in. I mean, they have so much more in common. But after everyone left, he walked me home, just the two of us, because Ingrid was staying overnight with Julie. When we got to my house, he kept talking, and we went inside, and I could tell he did not want to leave, but it was impossible for him to stay. I liked him so much. When he smiled at me I felt numb.

Peter says I am different from the other Danish girls he has met. I asked him how. He laughed and he stared at me and said, "Well, you laugh like other girls, and you are so Danish . . ."

I pretended to be annoyed, and I asked him what that means. He said, "Blond and tall and beautiful." He thinks I am beautiful! Does he really mean it? And then he said, "But you are always thinking and analyzing. Making plans. What will you do, Fredericka, when you are finished with school?"

And I told him I will be a writer. I have never told this to anybody before. Now that I have said it, for the first time it is beginning to seem real. I will be a writer. And then Peter wanted to know what I would write about, and I found myself telling him so many things.

With Peter I feel different. He thinks I am intelligent. I can tell by the way he listens to me. We talked about books, and I told him about Isak Dinesen and her books, mainly her life in Africa. Peter promised to read Out of Africa *as soon as he can. He wants to share it with me, he said.*

When I got up this morning, everything looked brighter, sweeter. I did not think it would happen to me so soon. In fact, I suppose I imagined it might never happen at all, and I would be this lonely, aging writer, sitting at my wooden desk composing wonderful stories from the imagination, and keeping a garden.

I did not realize I had this great need for conversation, and not just conversation, but with him. He listens to everything I say. He takes it in, thinks deeply about my words, as if they really matter. And then I want to explain things in a better, fuller way, because I can see that it really does matter now. We talked about everything—school and people and how they are, sometimes hypocritical, absurd, or haughty. He wants to know what I think about everything. When he looks at me, I see myself in his eyes, womanly and truly beautiful.

I have started to write another story. Peter says he wants to read my stories. Maybe I will show them to him—or maybe some of the poems. I have never known a boy who was really interested in literature. Or if they are, they seem so effeminate. Peter is not in the least effeminate.

We went to Tivoli. The girls came, too. They were so funny, giggling and whispering, watching me and Peter. So obvious! Niels wanted to come, and how could I say no? When Peter came to the door, the two of them went right to talking as if they'd known each other for years. Well, with Niels going, of course Emil had to come. That was quite another story. Emil, silly little monkey, chattering away, trying to impress Peter with his knowledge of boats and sextants and all those seafaring things that didn't interest Peter in the least. But he was polite and kind. It is more than I can say for Emil. I don't want to write about Emil!

Tivoli was extraordinarily beautiful. Peter took my hand when we walked past the tulips, so grand, so gorgeous. I have never seen them so pretty. We arrived just at dusk. The lights are not as bright as usual, because of the occupation and the blackouts. We have had to put blackout curtains on our windows. So ugly! But there were still a few lights strung around the pagoda, and the lights from the pantomime theater. I never realized how very beautiful it is; the lights look like stars come down to Earth. That is how I thought of it. We went on the Ferris wheel, and on the top I looked down and began to shiver. All of Copenhagen lay beneath us, the spires, the red rooftops, the twisted church tower, the large squares. How beautiful it is! Beyond I could see the sea and the ships. It is difficult to imagine that all this has been here, and I did not notice.

Peter put his arm around me. I was afraid to move; I wanted the moment to last. When we came down we walked very slowly together, and his arm was still around me. He bought us ices and cakes and chocolate—I'm afraid he doesn't have much spending money. I said I wasn't hungry, but he only laughed and kept buying sweets for me and the girls. Niels and Emil went their own way to the roller coaster—good riddance!

Peter and I sat on a bench and watched the people, and I have never been so absorbed in anything. Peter told me about his life in Czechoslovakia, how he had to leave, because everybody knew that Hitler was going to attack. At least he and his parents knew. Some people just blind themselves to reality. Peter isn't like that. He is so sensitive. A little boy lost his mother and sat crying on the path.

Peter went to him, spoke to him so kindly, and the mother came, and she was most grateful.

Peter said he will be coming to Copenhagen now quite often—something about getting supplies for the farm. He can drive the truck and also the tractor. Seems to me he can do just about anything. Peter says he would like to call me whenever he comes to Copenhagen. He asked me, would I mind?

Would I mind?

My heart is singing. Would I mind?

Chapter Seven

Letter from Willi

Liebe Mutti,

You will be happy to know that I'm well and safe here in Denmark.

My health improves daily, now that I am no longer on the front lines. I thank God for sparing my poor life while all around me comrades fell. I am trying to be worthy of this gift and to use it to promote all that we cherish.

Yes, I do feel pain in my knee at times, but it is not severe. I know that my pain is a small price to pay for the glory of our Führer. You cannot imagine how it was to come face-to-face with those Communists. They are barbarians.

I have been assigned to guard duty at the general headquarters, which is the first position for all new arrivals. Eventually I hope to become adjunct to one of the clerks or even to one of the ministers.

Since my arrival in Denmark two weeks ago, I believe I have gained eight kilograms, so do not worry that your son is starving. In fact, they call this "the whipped cream front." There is a special café-salon right opposite the railroad station, called Lido, where I and my comrades go for afternoon coffee and cake, with cream when it is available, and often for a supper of Danish delicatessen, which includes their wonderful herrings, dark bread with jam, ham, cheese, cucumbers, and tomatoes. How wise, how farsighted of our Führer to take this land under his protection. The Danes are a simple people, given to farming and small, light industry. With our organization and a governing hand, they can be made to produce most of the food we need not only for our army, but later, for all Germany. And what a relief it was to see people going about their business in proper fashion, the children hearty and fine looking, the women some of the prettiest I have ever seen. The girls wear their hair in braids, some of them bobbed in the new style; all ride bicycles, which gives a pleasant shape to the body and legs. Forgive me, Mother, but I am a man, and I notice these things, even though I am still and forever

Your son,
Willi

P.S. There is a street where we do not go, called Kogensgade. In fact, the café there is off-limits to us, and just as well. It is frequented by Jews. Some of the boys say those people won't be here for long.

P.P.S. How is my little Dodi? Are you keeping her clipped or shaggy? Please give her a special little treat and tell her it is from Willi.

Part Two

1941–1942

Chapter Eight

Niels

Sometimes Niels wished he were a better student. From the beginning, when he was seven and herded into the classroom for the first time, he didn't think he could bear it. All day indoors when he longed to be out with Emil! They were in the same class, but forbidden to talk, forbidden even to turn around and make motions to each other. It seemed unthinkable that his life, from now on, would be lived in this cage, this box of a room where they made children sit without moving or talking, except by permission.

In time, Niels grew accustomed to the discipline of school. But as he gazed out to the sky, he envied the birds and even the tree limbs their freedom.

And now it was summer. He and Emil had planned this for months. With their birthday monies they had bought a small tent. Sleeping bags would be donated by Emil's grandfather—two old woolen lumpy things with oilcloth bottoms, fine against the cool of summer nights on the seacoast. Niels's father had given them a small camp stove for cooking sausages and, if they were lucky, fresh fish. In the end, they each brought a can of beans and brown bread, some cheese, and, between them, one tomato, three apples, and a cucumber. They were off for the shore. Emil's grandfather, with a small house behind the dunes, near Helsinor, would greet them but let them go their own way. He was not one to spoil a boy's independence.

"Do you have any money?" Emil asked, tying the tent to the back of his bicycle with stout cord.

"A few kroner," replied Niels. "We can get some pastries on the way, okay?"

"Excellent! We'll stop at Jensen's."

"Take a raincoat!" shouted Emil's mother from the window.

"Who has a raincoat?" Emil called back. "You forget, Mor, mine fell apart last winter."

"Mine, too," said Niels. "My mother cut it down for Ingrid." He kicked at a spot on the pavement, feeling the hole in his shoe. "Have to get this repaired," he said morosely. "Or start wearing wooden clogs." A group of German soldiers walked by. "They have stolen everything," he said bitterly, "our food, our cloth, and shoe leather. We are like their personal warehouse—only they don't pay for anything."

"Look, this is our vacation. I'm tired of worrying about the Wehrmacht. Let's go to the bakery, then off! We have a long ride ahead of us."

"Do you have the fishing things?"

"Here in this pack. You take it. I have the tent. Come."

They rode down the street to the bakery. It was still early, and several housewives hurried to buy freshly baked bread and rolls for breakfast. The smell of sweet pastries was overpowering as Niels opened the door and walked up to the counter. The boys emptied their pockets, putting their coins onto the counter.

"Well, I have not seen you boys for a while!" exclaimed Bente Jensen, the owner. Her large bulk was wrapped in a long white apron. "*They* are collecting those copper coins now," she said with a grimace.

Emil thrust out his chin. "They want our money? How can we buy anything, then?"

"Replacing them with aluminum. They use the copper for war matériel, don't you know? Well, I'll take them. What do you boys want?"

"Half a dozen baker's sore eyes," Niels said, pointing to the pastries with the custard center and blob of red jelly. "My favorite," he said. Already, his mouth watered. "Mine, too," said Emil. "And get a loaf of that French bread."

Bente Jensen took the coins, counting them carefully. She sprang open the register and tucked in an IOU, keeping the coins in her hand. Conspiratorially she leaned across the counter, glanced about, then said, "These coins I put away into a special box. *They* won't get them. I save them for a later time." She winked and added softly, "What else can we do?"

Niels nodded. He had seen several girls wearing small copper coins around their necks, strung on narrow ribbons. Resistance, he told himself scornfully. What was the big deal? Hanging on to coins that the Germans wanted, wearing the red and white cap or the lapel pin with the king's insignia—all petty pranks. In the long run, it meant nothing. The Wehrmacht, with their pistols and rifles and high boots and tanks, laughed at the Dane's ridiculous antics.

"I put in a few extra pastries from yesterday, no charge," Bente Jensen called after them, and the boys called back their thanks.

Outside, they ate two pastries apiece. Niels saved the rest in his knapsack. "If we only had a motorcycle," he said, "we'd get there in less than two hours."

"You are dreaming again," said Emil.

"If we got jobs," said Niels, "we could combine our money and buy one together. A used one. Maybe a used Harley."

"Maybe," Emil conceded. "Let's go. Do you have your identity card?"

"Of course." Niels patted his shirt pocket. "Here."

"Let's go!"

They twisted and turned their way out of the city as the sun broke through the early morning mist. Niels took off his jacket and unbuttoned his shirt collar, to let sun touch his skin. By summer's end, he hoped, he would look tan and vigorous, like those American teenagers they used to see in the movies.

"Too bad there are no new films," he called back to Emil.

"What? You want to see a film? Do you have enough money?"

"No, never mind. I'm sick of German films—a lot of propaganda." He recalled the afternoons when he and the girls—Fredericka, Ingrid, and Julie—all went to the theater to see the American films. Julie insisted on seeing *Alexander's Ragtime Band* three times over. Now it was almost impossible to find such films playing anywhere; the Nazis censored everything.

"What?" Emil shouted.

"Nothing!" Niels called back. Out on the open road, the wind whipped at his hair, sunshine flickered into his eyes. He squinted at the elms that dripped with new pale green leaves, flashes of color, reminding him of the paintings that Ingrid made. Now she painted with swirls and drops of color, a big improvement over the boxlike houses and trees she used to draw as a little child. Well, she was turning into a young lady, after all. She had just had her confirmation last month. Such a flurry of giggles and clothes and excitement! He remembered his own confirmation two years ago. Ingrid's party was much smaller and quieter than his had been. Oh, there was the usual supper with fancy cakes and party favors. But the party ended early. With petrol so scarce, most people walked or brought bicycles, and they tried to avoid being in the streets at night. His sisters seemed to tolerate the restrictions better than he and Emil. Girls are more easygoing, he thought.

Fredericka lounged around in the afternoons, reading or repairing skirts on her sewing machine. She lived for the Sundays when Peter managed to get to Copenhagen on the train. Then Fredericka seized the bathroom for hours, getting ready. When she emerged, she usually looked no different than before. *Girls!* Tonight, lying under the stars, he and Emil would inevitably talk about girls.

For now, it was enough to feel the freedom of the day, the open road, the *whoosh* of the few cars that passed them, usually with occupants on serious errands. Nobody had gasoline to waste on holiday driving. Every turn, every thought brought home a single reality—occupation. The thought rarely left him, though Far discouraged talk about it. When Uncle Jens came, there was always a new joke, something that did the Nazis in, and a litany of complaints. Jens still wore the Danish police uniform, but his orders came from the German command. "Every morning we get directives," he told Niels. "Long lists of people we should watch and apprehend. Last week someone penciled in the names Hitler, Himmler, and von Ribbentrop!" He laughed.

It was high noon when Niels and Emil wound around the last turn and caught sight of the Kronborg Castle on the left, its green copper turrets rising to the very blue, cloudless sky. The castle sat in the middle of a spit of land, surrounded by the sea, impregnable. Legend told of Holger Danske, one of King

Charlemagne's knights, who became so homesick for his beloved Denmark that he walked all the way home from France. Exhausted, he laid himself down in the castle's lower chambers and fell asleep. He sleeps there still, but will rise to Denmark's aid if ever the country is attacked.

Dreaming, Niels might have veered off into the middle of the road. He would never know exactly how it happened, for Emil had gotten ahead of him by several meters. Next thing Niels knew, he heard the blast of a horn at his back, felt the wind of an automobile traveling so swiftly and so close, it seemed a miracle that he only lurched, then skidded into a ditch by the side of the road. Shocked by his fall, Niels barely saw the back end of a German car, and he clearly heard the taunting laughter of the soldiers.

He got up, shaken. His shirt was ripped at the elbow, his arms scraped from the gravel.

"What happened?" Emil called, turning back.

"Bloody Nazis!" Niels shouted.

"Did they dump you on purpose?"

Niels shook his head. "I don't know. Maybe not. Maybe it was just an accident."

"Well, come on. Don't let it spoil our day."

But the day was touched now by an ugliness, not the accident so much as the laughter. The soldiers seemed always to be laughing, as if here, in Denmark, they had caught the golden ring. They called it "the whipped cream front." They hung around the taverns with Danish girls. They swaggered and laughed on the streets of Copenhagen. Niels had hoped, somehow, that the countryside would be clear of them, and he could forget the occupation, for once.

Niels dusted himself off, irritated at his own foolish notion.

They were here, solid as leeches on a rock. His father counseled patience and calm. "Forget them," he said. "Just go on about your own business, Niels."

Niels did not argue, but every time his father gave such advice, it widened the rift between them. Why couldn't his father be more like Uncle Jens?

True to his hopes, the sea breeze, the sand dunes, and the shrieking gulls soon worked their magic. Emil's grandfather saw them off with a wave and bag of cherries, precious fruit he must have hoarded just for the boys.

"Can we take the boat out tomorrow?" Emil pleaded. "Just for a few hours?"

"No, Emil. It is not wise. They patrol the coastline."

"So? We have nothing to hide," Emil argued.

"Also, there are mines in some of the inlets."

"But the fishermen go out!" Emil said.

"They must make a living, so they take the risk. You boys will have to stay on shore, at least for now."

Emil got that dark look in his eyes. "I am not afraid," he argued.

"But I am," said his grandfather with a slight smile. "Old men do not have the courage of young boys. Go on, now. Have a pleasant time. Do you need matches?"

"We have them, sir," Niels answered. "Wish us luck and we may have a fish dinner."

"Good luck!" The grandfather stood waving, his weathered face reflecting many years, many memories. "Use the night crawlers!" he called.

It was one of those afternoons when time seemed to stretch, yet again all of it flew too swiftly—finding their campsite, setting up the tent, then hurling themselves into the foaming waves for a swim in the frigid water. Afterward they walked back along the dunes to their small camp, dried themselves off, and sat down amid several large boulders. The boulders had retained the noonday heat and warmed their backs pleasantly.

"Wish we had some beer," Emil said.

"Could we get some?"

"Maybe at the hotel," Emil said. "Any money left?"

"Enough for one bottle, maybe," said Niels, taking the coins from his pocket. To his surprise he found a bill in the small, hidden pocket at his waist. He waved it triumphantly. "Here! Two bottles, at least!"

"We'll go later, when it's crowded. They won't care about our age."

"Let's pull up the lines," Niels said.

"Patience," said Emil. "Wait awhile. You catch more fish by waiting." He nodded toward the long poles, baited with night crawlers strung along the line.

Emil reached into his shirt pocket and brought out two cigarettes.

"Where did you get those?" Niels asked.

"What do you care? You want one?"

"Sure."

They smoked, intent on the tobacco. Niels held the smoke in his mouth, sucked it slowly down into his chest, feeling the harsh, brittle heat. Niels hated the taste, but he liked the smell of the smoke, especially here, out in the open. There was something very strong, very masculine about it. He flicked away the ash, inhaled deeply, and coughed violently.

It sent Emil into spasms of laughter. Niels laughed with him and stubbed out the cigarette, which Emil retrieved to save in his pocket. Later, they hauled up their catch, fried the small fishes—there were seven of them—heated up the beans, pulled off chunks of French bread, and ate until they were stuffed.

The pale dusk hung over the horizon for hours. The sky would not really darken until ten or so. Meanwhile, they talked about everything, especially girls.

"Well, I do think Dagmar likes you," Niels insisted. "She is always hanging around looking at us."

"Dummy, it's you she is interested in. Anyhow, Birgit is more to my taste. I like girls that are not always talking. Birgit doesn't say much."

"She hasn't much to say—I think she is a little low on brains."

"You want a brainy girl?"

"Why not? Nothing wrong with brains. Look at Fredericka—she's always reading, and the boys love her."

"I don't love her." Emil's tone belied his words.

"Come on, you are crazy about her, and you know it."

"Is she still going around with that Jew?"

"What Jew?"

"The one who went with us to Tivoli."

"You mean Peter? The farmer?"

Emil ground out his cigarette, crossed his arms over his chest, demanding, "Are you dense, Niels? Don't you know he is a Jew? Can't you see it in his face?"

"I—I guess I never thought about it. What if he is?"

Emil pulled himself up and began to walk toward the village. "Forget it," he flung over his shoulder. "If you don't know, I'm not going to tell you."

"Why are you so irritated? What do you care who is a Jew or who is not? What have they ever done to you?"

"I have nothing against Jews," Emil said, walking swiftly. "But doesn't it strike you that they are always at the center of trouble?"

"Are you saying it's their fault the Nazis hate them?" Niels retorted.

"Oh, come on, Niels, you are so naive. Let's go get that beer. I'll buy it—you wait by the door, you and your baby face."

Niels felt the hot retort rising to his lips, but he held his peace. He hated it when they argued. Suddenly everything seemed spoiled, rotten.

They walked without speaking. Now the stars were popping out, and from the hotel came the sound of merriment. The windows were darkened with the required blackout curtains, but now and then a small stream of light shot out, like a bolt, quickly extinguished.

They walked up to the door of the tavern and in a moment were nearly blinded by light and smoke. It was hot from the crush of many bodies, mostly men enjoying their beer or something stronger. The few women at the round wooden tables were sitting very close to the soldiers or were perched on their laps, laughing and flirting with their eyes.

Niels felt his anger rising. How could Danish girls go out with these men—plunderers, invaders? And for what? A bar of chocolate, a pair of silk stockings? Or perhaps they simply loved a man in uniform. Damn them!

Emil stood at the bar, slamming his kroner down, brashly ordering three bottles of Tuborg.

Niels remained by the door, beside the coatrack with its layers of jackets and heavy woolen overcoats with the Nazi insignia on the collar. He glimpsed a patch of black leather, a buckle, the butt of a gun. One of them had hung his holster up under his coat!

Niels stared at the pistol, his heart thumping.

Men's laughter rang out, together with the high-pitched

giggle of a girl, then a combined shout: *"Prosit!"* The soldiers slapped the tabletop, flung out their legs, drank the Danish beer with all the gusto and arrogance of conquerors. Again their laughter boomed around him, like the laughter of the men who had almost hit him with their car. They wouldn't have cared if they'd killed him—they would have laughed.

Niels reached out. Swiftly he pulled the pistol from its holster and pushed it into his waistband, under his jacket. He felt its latent power, like a clenched fist against his belly.

Niels watched Emil come toward him, with the beer in a bag. On Emil's face was a proud, victorious smile.

Baby face, Emil had called him. Just wait until Emil saw this!

Chapter Nine

Julie

"Are you ready for a new piece, my friends?" Helga opened her briefcase and pulled out two books of new piano music. She turned to Ingrid. "I have a lovely little Beethoven piece for you," she said, smiling. "It is very famous. 'Für Elise.'"

"What about Julie's?" Ingrid asked.

"I have a new Chopin waltz for Julie. Don't look so sad, Ingrid! After all, Julie has been studying piano much longer than you. You're doing *fine.*"

"Will you play them for us?" They both crowded close to their young teacher.

"Of course," Helga said. She positioned her hands on the keyboard and sat for a moment, silent, eyes half closed, as if she were already listening to the music. Softly she began, the same two notes, then the run, each note flowing into the next as graceful as water cascading from a fountain.

"I'll never play it that well," Ingrid said.

"Of course you will," Helga said. "Now the Chopin. Follow the music, Julie. You can turn the page for me."

The light, beautiful strains of the waltz filled the room. The music seemed to blend with the deep red velvet draperies at the sides of the windows. The panes were darkened with black paper, a constant reminder of the danger of air raids and bombs. But now, as Helga played, Julie imagined the halls of Kronborg Castle with their gilded chandeliers, brocade chairs and marble floors, and beautiful people dancing. She loved Chopin, his music and his independent spirit.

"Now then," said Helga, buckling her briefcase. "Begin with the first page, each of you. Slowly, hands separately first, then together. Practice, Ingrid!" She chuckled and patted Ingrid's shoulder. "I know you are terribly busy with your schoolwork, and you have a few other things to do. Have you done any new paintings?"

"No. Paints and paper are so expensive now . . ."

"Like everything else," said Helga, walking to the door.

"We'll walk you to the bus," said Julie.

"Well—that would be nice."

"We're walking with Helga!" Julie called to Mrs. Giesler. "Shall we take Sammy with us?"

"I want to go!" yelled Sammy. He came running out, both hands outstretched, caked with mud.

"We've been planting," said Mrs. Giesler. "We must wash his hands first. If you are taking him," she added, "I will go home a little early today. Three big, strapping boys—you would think they know how to warm up a stew, eh? They still want Mama to feed them." She laughed and wiped Sammy's hands on a towel.

"It's fine, Mrs. Giesler," Julie said. She picked up a sweater for Sammy and wrote a note for her mother: "Took Sammy for a walk—we'll be back by five." Her mother usually got home from the library between five and six, unless there was an evening program. Nowadays there were few. People wanted to be home when it got dark.

Outside, the afternoon sun shone brightly, and Julie unbuttoned Sammy's shirt collar to let the sun touch his chest. Several mothers with babies in prams walked by, talking animatedly together. Julie remembered how tiny Sammy used to be. Now he let go of her hand and skipped just ahead, looking back, enjoying his freedom.

They hurried along, Helga and Ingrid talking, Julie watching Sammy as he scampered along with his three-year-old energy and curiosity. He hopped and ducked, picking up bits of things—a pebble, a coin, a candy wrapper.

"Sammy, you are a regular garbage collector!" Julie scolded, but she laughed as Sammy gleefully reached out toward a waddling, nodding pigeon that skillfully eluded his grasp.

The streets were filled with the usual afternoon cars, pedestrians, and bicycles. Shops did a brisk business in spite of the rationing; luckily, only a few items were scarce. Most of the complaints were about the ersatz coffee, horrible stuff brewed from acorns. Julie had never liked coffee anyhow. What she really missed were chocolates. They passed by the confectioners', and she yelled to Helga, "Wait up! I want to go in and get some candy." Sammy ran back at the word *candy,* his face bright with expectation.

But Helga suddenly turned back. Her eyes were terror-filled.

"What is it, Helga?" Julie called, but in the next moment she knew, for she was caught in a chaotic stampede, people racing toward them, shouting, throwing bottles and stones. Instinctively Julie pulled Sammy close, caught him up in her arms. He struggled and screamed, "Let me down! Let me down!" Julie clutched him all the tighter, turning this way and that, wildly seeking shelter. But there was none, only the increasing sound of trampling feet, the roar of voices pitched in angry revolt, the crash of objects smashing against cars and buildings, stopping people in their tracks.

"My God," Julie screamed. She backed away a few steps, but it was too late. Stones came hurtling through the air as the angry mob rounded the corner, herded like wild cattle by uniformed men, the Danish police in black, the Germans in green, using rubber truncheons and clubs and fists.

"Gestapo pig police!" screamed the demonstrators. "Filthy pigs!"

Julie turned, racing to shield herself and Sammy under an awning, poor protection against the debris that now flew past. The air was filled with screams and loud popping sounds, the roar of engines. Julie felt Sammy's body pressed against her. Her arms ached. Now Sammy clutched her so tightly she could hardly breathe. Fragments rained down upon them—glass and pebbles, foul eggs and trash, spattering against Julie's skin, her clothes. Sammy screamed and screamed. Julie felt a sharp pain, uncertain whether in his terror Sammy had bitten her or a bottle had struck her neck. She touched the spot and felt a sticky wetness. Blood.

Beside her, Ingrid was crying. Helga's face looked frozen. The four of them stood huddled together against the human storm all around.

"No more arrests! No more arrests!" screamed the rioters, students from the university. "Gestapo pig police!" they shouted. "Free Denmark!"

A police car careened around the corner, followed by half a dozen others, all with sirens wailing. Still Sammy screamed, and Julie stood pressed against the wall, afraid to move, afraid to stay, unable to make sense of it. "Sammy, shhh," she called out continually. "I have you. It's all right. Hush. Hush."

A group of green-clad German soldiers leaped from truck to street, throwing up a barricade of boxes and planks, and, finally, the trucks themselves. The soldiers stood in front of their barrier, rifles drawn, faces full of hate and fury. People, young and old, scattered in every direction.

Helga clutched her briefcase to her chest, like a shield. Sammy whimpered, kicking his legs against Julia's stomach. "Stop it! Stop it, Sammy!" she shouted, then kissed his wet cheeks, his sleek hair. "Hush, hush, baby. Look, it's only trucks, big trucks. Nothing to worry about. I'm here."

"What's happened?" Ingrid shouted. "What is it all about?"

A man who had taken refuge beside them shouted to Ingrid. "They hate the Communists. In every country they occupied, the Nazis hounded out the Communists, along with the Jews."

"But why?" Ingrid screamed back.

Her words were lost in a new wave of violence.

"If they arrest the Communists today," the man shouted, "who will be next?"

Julie shuddered at the absurdity of it, the horror of it. All this turmoil here in Copenhagen, because the Germans hated the Russians? How could such things happen? She wanted to scream out, "We are innocent!" But who would listen?

The students gathered for another assault on the barricade. Danish and German police met them head on, swinging their truncheons, beating people on the back, the shoulder, the head. One boy fell on the street, was pulled up again and beaten down to the ground. Blood streamed from the boy's forehead, into his eyes.

A rifle was fired. Julie turned to face the wall, shielding Sammy with her body. And as she felt the cold, wet surface against her cheek, with the chaos all around, two words formed in her mind, *Dear God,* over and over. *Dear God . . .*

In a moment's hiatus, she turned again and saw two young men carrying a girl away. Her arms hung down limply; her head rolled to one side.

"We have to get out of here," Helga moaned.

A German officer bolted toward them, stopping in front of Julie as if he had been watching her, singling her out. She almost screamed. She had never been so close to a German soldier before. She could see the pale mole on his upper lip and the coldness in his gray eyes. "What are you doing here?" he shouted. His hand swung out as if he meant to strike her. "You bring your child to such a place—what are you doing?"

Julie's knees trembled. Her heart pounded in her throat, her chest. Did he think she had come into this madness on purpose? Was he crazy? Fury made her bold.

"He is not my child. He is my brother!" she shouted angrily. "How could I help it? We were just walking." A terrible, inexplicable rage pounded through her. "Help us get out of here!" she demanded.

The soldier took a step closer, so that she felt his breath on her face. "Silence!" he commanded. "Your papers."

Sammy, in her arms, was immobile, a deadweight. Julie felt his fear and a hot wetness seeping down the side of her skirt.

"It's all right," Julie breathed. She glanced at Helga, who stood there still clutching her briefcase, her face ashen.

"Here is my student card. Let us pass," Julie said, drawing herself up, attempting to mimic her mother's domineering tone. "We have to go home. We are not involved in this. We are only in middle school."

"Silence!" he shouted again, jabbing his finger at Julie. "I want to see papers for all of you. Now!"

"I told you, we are only in middle school." Julie moistened her lips. She attempted a smile. She knew that Ingrid had her student identification card. But Helga—what about Helga?

Something sped past them. A bottle crashed on the cobblestones at their feet.

The soldier's hand was on the butt of his pistol as he confronted Helga. "Identification. *Rasch!"*

Helga reached into her briefcase. Her trembling fingers drew out a mass of papers, scattering them onto the cobblestones. Sheets of music drifted up and were scuttled along in a sudden burst of wind. Helga's eyes seemed blinded, somehow, as she groped in the briefcase, then fumbled through her purse. Julie saw the pulse beating at the side of her face, saw how deathly pale her lips had become.

Suddenly another man rushed up, a Danish policeman, dressed in the black uniform. "Ingrid!" he called. "Julie, what on earth are you doing here?"

"Jens!" Ingrid screamed out. "Uncle Jens!"

Jens turned to the German, his tone brisk, laced with authority. "Is something the matter? Look, man, they are only children."

"This one has no papers," retorted the Nazi with a jerk of his head.

"Well, I will tell you," said Jens smoothly. "This is my niece and her friends. They belong at home. I will get them out of here immediately."

"This one must show me her papers," the German insisted, pointing to Helga. "Maybe she is a Communist. They are all to be arrested. It is an order from the commandant. Don't you know it? You are a policeman!" he said. "You are pledged to uphold the law!"

"But look, this child is bleeding. Let me take them home. I will take the responsibility."

"We have procedures." The soldier stood firm. "Orders."

"But I can vouch for this woman!"

"It is not enough for one Dane to know another. You think all we need is *your* approval?"

"But she is not a Dane!" Ingrid blurted out. "Helga is from Germany."

Instantly the man's eyes narrowed. "You are German? Then you are under my jurisdiction! Show me your papers!"

Slowly Helga handed him her identity card. She clenched her teeth and wiped her hand on her skirt.

The officer looked at the card, then at Helga. Stiffly he said, "You must come with me."

"Why must she?" Jens argued. "What is the matter? Look, I can be responsible . . ."

"You wish to be responsible for a German citizen? How do we know she is not a Communist? And she is a Jew. They are all Communists."

"I want your name," Jens shouted at the German. "You can be sure I will report this to the authorities."

The man clicked his heels. "You must do your duty," he said in a loud, stiff tone. "As I do mine." He grasped Helga's arm and pulled her away to a car. They were lost in the melee.

Jens took Sammy from Julie's arms. "Come, hurry," he said. They pushed their way through the crowd to Jens's patrol car. Julie, Ingrid, and Sammy squeezed together in the front seat. Exhaustion suddenly overcame Julie. All she could think about was sleep, silent sleep. She drew a deep breath, turned her head slightly.

In the backseat were four students, three boys and a girl. A red-haired boy was holding his elbow. Whenever the car hit a bump, he grimaced, gritting his teeth. "I think it's broken, Jacob," said the girl beside him. "Try not to move it." Her thin wrists stuck out from her dark sweater. Her face was pale, except for a bruise on her cheek and a deep scratch on her lip.

"Where are you taking us?" the girl asked brashly. She dabbed at her lip with the end of her sweater. In her gaunt face, her eyes looked very large and dark. There were deep smudges beneath them.

"You kids better get to a clinic," Uncle Jens told them grimly.

One of the boys rasped, "Aren't you taking us to prison?" His Adam's apple bobbed up and down, and he shivered.

"I am going to leave you off at the hospital," said Uncle Jens. "Ask for Dr. Ganz. Tell him Jens, the policeman, sent you."

They stopped at the clinic. The four leaped out with furtive looks, as if they expected to be shot. "Thank you! Thank you!" they called. "We will never forget you!"

Julie stared at Jens. His handsome profile was stern, his eyes straight ahead.

"You let them go!" She marveled.

Jens smiled. "Of course. I don't put kids in jail."

"Are they really Communists?"

Jens shrugged. "What if they are? What is a Communist? Someone who thinks the government should give everybody what he needs and the state owns everything. It sounds wonderful. Trouble is, there are always thugs and greedy officials to skim off the cream."

"I heard they kill everyone who doesn't agree with them," said Ingrid. "Just like the Nazis."

"You're right," said Jens. "What a world! You kids should be at the movies, not worrying about riots and killing."

At last they were back at Ingrid's house. Julie telephoned her mother. She came rushing over, anguished over Sammy, the cut on his forehead, the state of his clothes, wet and filthy. But he lay curled up, asleep on the sofa.

Julie explained everything—the riot, Uncle Jens's sudden appearance, Helga's arrest.

"What's going to happen to her?" Ingrid moaned. Her eyes were puffy from crying. "Why did I have to open my mouth? Why did I have to say she was German? What will they do to her?"

"We don't know anything yet," said her mother. "Jens has gone over to the German police station to try to find out what's happening. If they do not help, he will go to the Gestapo. Jens usually gets his way, whether with charm or threats. Don't worry."

Julie's mother sat down on the sofa beside Ingrid. "You didn't cause any of this, Ingrid," she said softly. "You didn't tell that German anything he would not have found out a minute later."

"I hate my big mouth!" Ingrid cried, sobbing again.

"It wasn't your fault, Ingrid!" Julie said. "Anyhow, what difference does it make? Your uncle Jens will take care of it. Helga is not a Communist. She hasn't done anything wrong. She's just a piano teacher."

But in her own mind, Julie was not convinced.

All night Helga was in Julie's thoughts, even while she slept. Immediately after breakfast, she ran over to Ingrid's house. Jens was there, sober, looking as if he had not slept at all.

"Thank you for saving us yesterday," Julie said.

He sighed and ran his hands through his hair in a desperate gesture. "I have tried everything in my power," he said in a voice rough with fatigue and frustration. "And I failed. They know she is Jewish. Since she is not a Danish citizen, we can't keep her here. They have sent Helga back to Germany. God only knows what will happen to her there."

The words spun through Julie's mind, and the nagging question: *If God knows, if God is there, how can He let this happen?*

CHAPTER TEN

Fredericka's Diary

There was a terrible riot, blood on the streets, soldiers, shooting.

Peter says it is a very bad sign that they have arrested the Communists. After all, they are just a political party, like the Social Democrats or even the Nazi Party. But now they have made the Communist Party illegal and arrested everyone. They were taken to Horserod Prison. Peter says it could have been worse. If they had been taken to Germany, they would be in concentration camps.

The things Peter told me about those camps are hard to believe. But he must know. Some of his family and friends from his village were sent to Dachau and some to another place called Buchenwald. The people have to work as slave laborers. Many of them starve to death or are beaten to death. Peter says there are international agencies, like the Red Cross, that check on such things.

It is getting tense here. One can feel it in the streets. I hate the way the Germans stare at us and call out. They try to approach us.

Peter says they are getting bolder now because they have attacked Russia, and they are winning.

It is dangerous for him here. Now that the German occupation has outlawed the Communists and arrested them, Peter says the Jews could be next. And not only is he a Jew, but he is also a foreigner—double trouble for him. Who will protect him? Nobody could protect poor Helga, Ingrid's piano teacher, because she was not a Danish citizen. I ask Peter what he is going to do. He only shakes his head and changes the subject.

I know he dreams constantly of going to Palestine. He has told me about it, even described it in detail, although he has never been there. I suppose he has seen it in his dreams—low hills covered with fig trees, deserts where nomads still tend their goats and sheep, and old Roman towns by the sea. "We will make it bloom again," he tells me, and his eyes shine. Oh, I do so love those dark, dark eyes, the way his mouth moves when he talks. He is not like anyone I have ever known. He is so very smart. He speaks German and Danish and Russian besides his own language. He can even read in English.

We are reading a book by Hemingway together. It is called A Farewell to Arms. *It is very sad, very good. Somehow everything we do is touched by war. Peter translates the words I do not understand. My English is not as good as his.*

I told him to read Isak Dinesen, and he did. He says she is a wonderful writer, so poetic, one can almost see and smell and taste the things she describes. I have told him about Isak Dinesen, who is Karen Blixen in real life, a baroness. He found it fascinating that Uncle Jens actually met her once at her home in Rugstedlund.

I read Out of Africa *again, and I imagined I was Karen Blixen, traveling to a strange, exotic land to be with my lover. I believe one must try to experience everything in life and not be afraid. Especially, one must not be afraid of change if one is to make the most of one's time on earth. K.B. proves that women can do anything, are capable of anything these days. She was a pioneer in Africa, totally out of her element, taking charge of a coffee plantation, and she made a great success of herself.*

I bought a book about Palestine. It has wonderful photographs and sketches.

I think it is important for a writer to experience all aspects of the world, to travel, to learn about different people, and not to get stuck in the same place all her life. I think a writer has to be willing to take risks.

CHAPTER ELEVEN

Niels

Niels kept the German pistol in an old tackle box in the back of his closet. He made it a rule never to look at it in the daytime. It was simply too dangerous. Anyone might walk in on him, especially Ingrid, the snoop. She was always hunting for things to use in her collages, bits of colored paper, clips, seashells, buttons. Privacy meant nothing to her. Niels had wanted to get a lock for his room, but Mor was adamantly against it.

"When you are all grown and move to your own place," she declared, "then you can lock your door. Until then, Niels, you are part of this household, and we do not lock each other out."

The pistol was like another person, a presence in his room. It weighed on his mind. Niels began to awaken in the deep night, when everyone was sleeping. Then he would switch on the lamp and move to the closet, open the tackle box, and take out the gun. It was a Walther P-38, heavy in his hand, cold and smooth. To Niels, it was a thing of beauty by virtue of its utter perfection. The gun could do exactly what it was meant to do. Its design was perfect, sturdy in the hand but not too heavy, small enough to be concealed, large enough to kill.

As he sat on the floor, cross-legged, with the gun in his hand,

Niels tried to imagine the pistol's history. Pictures flooded through his mind, of target practice, of real encounters, threats, and the final act, the slow pressure of the trigger finger, the swift release, and then *bam!* Someone who had been alive and breathing a moment earlier was now dead.

To hold this power in his hand was an awesome thing. He pulled back the slide, peered at the bullet in its ready position. With his thumb he unlatched the magazine from the handle, slid it out, and counted the seven remaining bullets. Once the trigger was set, the shots could continue until the magazine was empty. Eight bullets. Eight hits. People, not objects.

He had not told Emil about the pistol. On the way back from the pub, Emil had already consumed one of the beers. He was posturing in that crazy way of the mildly drunk, laughing and singing, talking about the girls he would charm. "If I had a uniform," Emil sang out, "then they would want me, don't you see? Women love a uniform. Didn't you see them in that tavern, how they hung on the soldiers? I tell you, they love the strap and the gun and the idea of violence. Oh, they pretend to be all softness and heart, sighing and squealing at the sight of a bug. What they really want is someone tough and strong."

They arrived at their campsite and lay back on their sleeping bags. Emil broke open another bottle of Tuborg, handing it to Niels, and he took a long pull from the third bottle. "If I had a uniform . . ." Emil went on.

"How would you get a uniform?" Niels had asked. "You want to be a policeman? Like my uncle Jens?"

"Ha! No, I am talking about the army. Haven't you heard? They are planning a Danish Free Corps, to fight on the eastern front."

"You mean against Russia? You mean, fight *with* the Germans?"

"Well, they are against Communists, and so are we, aren't we? Who do you hate more, the Germans or the Communists?"

"I—I don't know," Niels said. "I have never thought about it."

"It won't be as if I were in the German army, exactly. The Danish Corps will be separate, all Danes."

"But how could you march and fight under the German flag? And don't you have to be eighteen to join the corps?"

"I am tall for my age."

Niels took a long swallow of the beer. Several fireflies floated before him in the darkness. He watched their meandering ascent. "You mean, you would lie? You think you can get away with it, Emil?"

"What's the harm in trying?" Emil had said, laughing. "Come with me, Niels!" he cried. "Just think of it! We can go together."

"No!" The word burst out of him, harsh as a slap.

"Well, you probably wouldn't make it anyhow," Emil said, leaning back, tipping his head to finish the beer. "You and that baby face of yours."

Niels had leaped to his feet, furious, shouting. "You would fight with the Nazis? Betray your friends? Your country?"

"You make everything so black and white, Niels!"

"It is!" Niels had shouted back. He felt lost; his best friend was like a stranger.

Now Niels fingered the smooth lines of the pistol. It was cool to his touch. How would it feel if it were fired? It would surely be hot. The spent shell would eject. When all the shells had been fired, how would he find more ammunition? He supposed he could get it from Uncle Jens. How? Steal it, perhaps, from his uncle's supply? His uncle was meticulous with his things. Nothing was ever left unguarded. In the last few months Jens had frequently spent the night here, sleeping on the pullout sofa in the parlor. His extra uniform, underclothes, and boots were kept in a large chest beside the sofa. And the chest was locked. Uncle Jens saw to that, having brought his own padlock and key.

Ingrid had tried to poke her nose into it and failed. "Why is Uncle Jens spending more time here now?" she asked.

"What's the matter, you don't like my brother here?" Mor had asked testily.

"Of course!" cried Ingrid, mollified. "I just wondered. At Grandmother's house he has his own room. I love Uncle Jens, but sometimes I can't even listen to the radio because he is sleeping in the living room."

Mother had given her a steady stare of disapproval, mouth down.

"It's just a bit crowded here now," Ingrid had said lamely.

"When there is room in the heart," Mor quoted, "there is room in the house. *Shame* on you, Ingrid."

It was Mor's worst reprimand, implying a depth of humiliation that touched not only oneself and the present time, but one's whole upbringing and ancestry.

Now Niels sat with the gun on his lap, then sighed deeply and tucked it into his belt. It was his, his alone. He had decided that night, out under the stars, to keep this to himself, to trust no one, not even Emil. Especially not Emil, with his beer and his talk of violence. He had been gripped with an odd, empty feeling, a loss.

Carefully, noiselessly, Niels opened the window. The night was freezing but clear. Niels stuck his head out, inhaling the frosty air that stung his lungs and slapped against his cheeks. It was going to be a cold winter. Some old-timers predicted it would be a record breaker, with icicles already hanging from the eaves, though it was still early in November.

Niels pulled on his boots and his jacket, put his leg over the windowsill, and slipped outside onto the hard ground. He waited for a moment, then pulled the window down, leaving enough space to squeeze his fingers underneath it later.

Out alone in the darkness, he was overwhelmed with a surge of freedom and power. The gun in his waistband was like a protector, an invisible giant walking beside him. His steps felt light; he imagined that he was floating, soaring, a kind of guardian on a special mission—and he was.

He had noticed his target a few days before. It was a small thing, so simple and really insignificant, except in the matter of principle and morale. Anything that would aggravate and demoralize the Germans was important. Last week, his mother had sent him to the butcher to pick up a precious loin of pork, long ordered and awaited. The butcher, usually accommodating, had grumbled and grudgingly brought out a piece of mutton, gray with age and sticky to the touch. Furious, Niels rejected it with a shake of his head and a scornful grunt. "We do not eat rotten meat, thank you, sir!"

"Who do you think you are, young scamp?" the man called after him, enraged. "This is wartime! We take what we can get. Don't you think I would like fresh meat, too? They have it all! *They have it all!*"

Niels had walked away, his heart pounding with anger. A small sack of sugar hung from his hand. It had taken all their combined ration coupons to buy it. And then he spotted a German army truck parked beside an inn, not straight, but angled into a narrow alleyway, as if the driver sought to conceal it. Casually Niels walked up to the truck, glancing at the windows of the inn.

Yes, the soldiers were inside. They were up to some mischief, he was certain of that. Glancing about, Niels opened the sack of sugar. He sidled up to the truck, leaned across so that his jacket concealed the workings of his hand as he twisted off the gas cap and swiftly poured in nearly half the sugar.

He stopped, imagining consequences, discovery, being seized and beaten. But nothing happened. No sound came from inside the inn. The afternoon air was heavy with mist and chill, the streets nearly empty. A single passerby hurried on, without even a glance.

Quickly Niels replaced the gas cap and nonchalantly walked away. It had been so amazingly simple! The soldiers would be furious when they discovered the damage, for the truck would stall, the sugar having burned inside the engine. Likely, too, they would be punished for having left the truck unattended.

Niels had felt the same wave of excitement he was feeling now. He walked swiftly through the dark streets with the pistol in his belt, the matches and the bag in his pocket. Elation grew within him, like its own small flame, nurtured by each step toward the special field postbox, where German soldiers posted their letters home.

All was dark and silent. Cars were strictly forbidden at night, except for the most urgent errands of doctors or undertakers. Even stray cats were hunkered down against the cold.

There it stood, conspicuous, a large wooden box set into a post, painted white with the words diagonally in black block letters: DEUTSCHE WEHRMACHT POST.

Carefully Niels took the bag from his pocket. He held his breath against the smell of the kerosene soaked cotton. It had not taken much, poured from his father's gasoline can, to saturate the cotton. He stuffed the wad into an empty tobacco box. Since tin was no longer available, tobacco was packed in boxes, much to the disgust of smokers, who claimed their product grew stale. It was perfect for Niels's purposes. He struck the match, touched it to the side of the box and tossed the burning thing into the slot.

He stood aside for a moment, reluctant to leave. He heard a crackling sound, then a slight thud as the wood caught and burned. Then he hurried into the shadows and made his way slowly back, grinning with huge satisfaction as the smell of smoke reached him. He turned once and saw the glow of flames against the sky. It was a small fire compared with the conflagration he would like to have started, but it was a message.

He trotted the last block toward home, locating his own house by a combination of instinct and habit, for everything was dark.

Niels raised the window and hoisted himself up, one leg over the sill, pulling his body all the way inside. He reached for the lamp, when he felt an arm under his throat, and he was pulled to the floor. In panic, he gasped. A strong hand pressed down over his mouth.

"Shut up! Don't make a sound, you idiot. Wait. Let me pull down the shade."

Uncle Jens, fully dressed in his police uniform, crouched on the floor beside him, peering out through a slit in the window. "Did anybody follow you? See you?"

"No! What are you talking about! I just went out to—to bring the cat in. The cat got out somehow, and I . . ."

"Don't try to lie to me." Jens grasped his hand, turned it over, held it to his nose. "You think I don't know the smell of kerosene? What have you been up to?"

"Nothing. *Nothing.*"

"You just let the cat out." Jens's face was a study of restraint, his tone thick with sarcasm. "You got all dressed in boots and a jacket—what's that?" In one motion Jens reached out and took the pistol from Niels's belt. His breathing was rapid, and he bit his lip in consternation. "Now, this is something entirely different. We have to talk about it, Niels. Do you know what this means?" He held the gun down, pulled back the slide, peered into bullet chamber. "It's loaded," he muttered.

Niels said, "Of course. Semiautomatic. The clip is full, too."

Jens gave him a sharp glance. "Do you realize that for owning this, they would kill you?"

"This is a war," Niels said. "You always taught me to defend myself."

"Yes, when you were a child and bullies picked on you at school."

"Now the bullies are all over Denmark," Niels replied.

"A gun is not a toy."

"I am no longer a child. I might still need to defend myself."

"And what good is it to you?" Jens inquired softly, gravely. "Do you know how to use it?"

"Yes."

"How do you know?"

"I have studied it. I unhook the safety catch first, aim, pull the trigger. It will kick a bit. I must steady it with two hands. Aim for the chest. If it shoots high, he will get it in the head. If low, the groin. Effective, either way."

"So, you are quite an authority on guns," said Jens. "And the bomb? You made a kerosene bomb?"

"Just cotton and kerosene, to burn down the German mailbox."

"Ah. Ingenious."

"Are you going to tell Far?" Niels asked.

"What do you think?"

"I think we are on the same side. Ingrid told me how you let those students go."

"Yet you did not ask me anything about it," mused Jens. He sat down on Niels's bed, motioning for Niels to sit beside him. "How come you said nothing?"

"In these times," Niels said carefully, "it is better not to ask questions or to trust anybody."

"Even your own flesh and blood?"

Niels nodded. "Not even your best friend."

Jens nodded and sighed deeply. Slowly, his eyes upon Niels, he handed back the pistol. "I think I have some work that would interest you," he said. "Since your lips are sealed, I need not tell you that complete silence is vital. I will tell you nothing, Niels. Is it agreed?"

"Yes." Niels took the pistol and put it carefully back into the tackle box. He shoved the box to the back of his closest, concealed by clothing. "What do you want me to do?"

"Some papers need to be delivered. I will tell you where to get them. You must memorize the addresses. Never write anything down. Now, good night."

Niels stood up, conscious of the fact that his uncle was nearly a foot taller than he. It seemed incredible that he was to be his uncle's ally in a fight that nobody had defined and nobody really sanctioned. And, he wondered, were there many others like him and Jens?

His uncle turned back, whispered, "Next time you use the cat for an excuse, be sure to have her in your room at the start. Don't you know that cat is fast asleep under my feather bed?"

"How did you know I had gone out?" Niels asked.

Jens chuckled. "I just came in myself," he said. "I saw you

climb in the window." He held up his hand and smiled. "Remember! No questions."

"No questions," Niels echoed.

His father was always talking about compliance and negotiation. "We do not like it, but it is better than all-out war," he said.

Niels kept his arguments to himself. But no matter what his father said, he *was* waging a war. And now he had an ally.

Chapter Twelve

Julie

If only Helga were here . . . The thought had crossed Julie's mind a hundred times since Cousin Boris approached her with the idea. A Sunday concert in the park—singers on the stage, a grand sing-along, the sort of festive, patriotic affair that not only filled summer afternoons with music, but created a special bond among the people.

"You shall play at the *allsang,"* Cousin Boris declared, chewing on his battered cigar. "I have arranged it all. I know the sponsor, and I told him all about you, Julie, how talented you are, how beautifully you play."

Julie's mother stood by, astonished. "Why, Boris, what a wonderful opportunity! How ever did you arrange it?"

"Tut, tut, I know people, Edith," Boris said with a grin.

"I'm not that good, Cousin Boris," Julie objected. "I'm not a prodigy, far from it."

Michael said, "Now, Father, maybe Julie does not want to play in public. You cannot force her."

"Listen, I know what the people want," countered his father. "Julie is a wonderful Danish girl, a lovely girl like their own daughters. She doesn't need to be a musical genius! I have heard you play Chopin—you have the feel for it. Chopin created the 'Polonaise' in his love for his land. What rousing music! Filled with patriotic fervor! That is what you must bring to the people."

Julie's face felt flushed with the praise and the possibility. She called Ingrid immediately. "Ingrid! I have news."

"So, you heard about the reprisals." There was a tremor in Ingrid's voice.

"What reprisals? What are you talking about?"

"Didn't you hear? Saboteurs blew up a spare parts factory. The Germans had been waiting for those parts for months. They were so angry that they took three doctors and three nurses from Bispebjerg Hospital and shot them—to teach us a lesson, they said."

"But—how could they? Your father . . ." She hardly dared to ask. "Is he all right?"

"Far is all right. But he knew one of the nurses. She was a surgical nurse and worked with him. Mother knew her, too. It's horrible, but Far said we must not worry. It was one of those random things."

"Random," Julie repeated. "Yes." It was all random, who would live and who would die, who would fight and who would remain passive.

"What did you call about? You said you had news."

"It's—well, I'm playing at the *allsang,*" Julie said reluctantly. All the joy of it was gone.

But Ingrid said excitedly, "Really! Oh, Julie, how wonderful. Who is coming? What will you wear?"

"It's not important what I wear."

Ingrid protested, "You can wear my new white blouse, the one I wore for confirmation. Remember, Fredericka sewed on those beautiful pearl buttons? I insist!"

The next day Ingrid came over with the blouse carefully wrapped in tissue paper. It seemed like old times, laughing and planning together. "Julie, you'll be famous," Ingrid said. "Everyone will want to meet you. Probably they will put your name in the newspapers. Just think! Everyone is coming," she continued. "Fredericka has invited Peter. We're all getting there two hours early so we can sit on the grass right in front. Niels is bringing his camera. Will you pin up your hair? Let me do it for you," Ingrid begged. "We'll do it in an upsweep, like Hedy Lamarr in that crime movie *Algiers.*"

Julie laughed. "Sure. I'll look exactly like her!" She wished she could be more like Ingrid, floating through life, not letting anything really touch her. Even her paintings were soft and ethereal, with fairylike figures floating in a pale sky or sitting amid fields of pink and yellow flowers.

From the hall they heard a soft clattering. "Mail!" Sammy shrieked, racing to the door. Julie ran after him, catching sight of the mailman's red uniform as he strode past their window.

"Sammy, don't take the mail!" Julie shouted. "Remember what Mama said—don't tear anything!"

But it was too late. Sammy had scooped up all the letters and began ripping them open.

"Sammy! Stop it!" Julie shouted.

She grabbed the letters. Usually she pacified Sammy by handing him an advertisement, his own "mail." Now she stood silent, staring at the letter with international postage and the red-and-white airmail emblem. She saw the return address: International Red Cross.

"What is it?" Ingrid was beside her, looking over her shoulder.

"Mail! Mail!" cried Sammy, jumping up and down, tugging at Julie's shirt.

"Shut up, Sammy!" Julie shouted, giving him a kick, as if he were a dog at her heels. Sammy recoiled. He crouched on the floor, his face red, his body rolled into a ball and rocking, whimpering.

"Sammy, I'm"—Julie's breath caught in her throat as she read the letter, and she whispered—"sorry. So sorry."

Her eyes scanned the message a second time. ". . . regret to inform you that the two persons in question, Helga Friedeman and Hanna Friedeman, have been deported to Auschwitz concentration camp. Unfortunately, it is impossible at present to discover the disposition of . . ." She let the letter drop.

Ingrid picked it up. She read the words. She stood staring at Julie.

"What does it mean?" Ingrid whispered at last.

"It is a death camp," Julie whispered.

"How—why this letter to you?"

"It's to my mother. She had inquired through the Red Cross. The Germans keep lists. They are very good at keeping lists. Meticulous."

"And who is Hanna?"

"Helga's mother. They were taken together." Julie turned to look at Ingrid's face, a study in confusion. "Haven't you heard about this?" she asked, her voice rising. "Don't you know what they do to people?"

Ingrid shook her head. Julie saw tears in her friend's eyes. She did not want to tell her. Why not leave her in ignorance? Why burden her with this awful truth? But relentlessly, as if driven, Julie began. She knew everything. She had overheard her parents talking. And there was literature from the library and the Jewish Community Center, pamphlets and articles with excruciating detail, numbers and locations and then, always, the unanswerable questions: What now? How can we save ourselves? Where do we go for help?

She said, "People are taken to these camps in cattle cars. Even children are taken, even little babies. They are packed into the trains, the sides are boarded up. They cannot escape! They have no toilets—you can imagine how it is. No water or food. Some die on the way. The others must live with the corpses. They get there and the doors are pried open. The Nazis pull them out. They have guns and whips and dogs to keep the people in line. Someone decides who will live—who will die. Those chosen to live become slaves, doing terrible, hard labor. Those who will die are taken to a shower room, naked, and then—"

"Stop it!" Ingrid screamed. "It isn't true! It cannot be true, Julie!"

Julie looked up to see her mother in the doorway. "Julie!" she cried. "What in God's name are you telling her?"

For a long moment everyone froze. "The truth," Julie said. A terrible burden lay upon her. "The truth."

◆ ◆ ◆

The afternoon was bright with a clear blue sky. Puffs of wind had scoured away every last cloud. The breezes blew small elm and aspen leaves through the air, like pale green confetti. All night long Julie's sleep had been a tunnel of horrors, images of Helga accosted by large dogs, Helga torn from her mother's embrace, Helga calling out, "Be happy, children! Be happy." Between the scenes came the music, weirdly distorted, a piano gone out of control. Then came visions of Ingrid, her face, flat and disbelieving, utterly stunned. And she felt guilty and vicious for what she had done to her friend.

She woke up, exhausted and determined. Only music could help her now.

The morning passed in a haze—breakfast, scales on the piano. Ingrid came to do her hair, but they decided to leave it as it was, natural and plain.

"I'm sorry, Ingrid, about how I hurt you," Julie told her friend.

"What's there to apologize about? Nothing!" Ingrid tossed her head. "Come on, it's a long walk to the park. And you have to be there early."

They walked, joining crowds of people, young mothers with babies in prams, old people with canes, students and shopkeepers, everyone streaming toward the park. Julie's parents and cousins walked with them. "What a day, what a beautiful day," Julie's father kept saying, nodding to people as they went. Julie felt his pride. Her hands began to sweat. Stage fright always struck her before a recital. Today, it was more than that. It was a test. Even as she walked and talked and smiled at passing strangers, another refrain spoke in her mind. *Please—make my hands steady. Help me to play my best. Not for me, but for the people. Help me, grant me this. Please.*

Grandmother Sophie came with her friends. The three elderly ladies sat on folding chairs, wearing capes and shawls around their shoulders. The park was packed with people, pressing toward the bandstand, pressing against the fenced perimeter and trailing out to the street.

Not for me, Julie told herself, waiting in the shade of the bandstand as everyone gathered. *Not for me, or even for the singing. They come for Denmark, to show unity, to sing out for freedom.* For, indeed, groups of German soldiers were crowded in among the Danes, and some stood guard at the gates, as they spied on every gathering, showing their might and their authority.

It began, of course, with the national anthem: "There Is a Lovely Land." Julie felt shivers running down her back as hundreds of voices combined, ringing out beyond the trees, embracing one another. Then came the song leader, a popular male singer beloved and adored. They sang the old songs, songs of the sea and the broad farmlands, songs of conquest and victory and freedom.

The German soldiers stood by, mute and uncomprehending. Some swayed their heads or tapped their feet in innocent unity with their foes. The song leader announced a flute solo. A young man played brilliantly. And then . . .

"Miss Julie Weinstein . . . the 'Polonaise' by Chopin."

The piano stood open on the stage, like a huge black bird with its wing lifted. The expanse of white keys seemed to beckon to her, waiting like old friends for her touch.

Julie paused, as Helga had taught her to do, letting the music mood envelop her completely, thinking only of music, music. Then, lifting her hands high over the keys, she let drop the first chord, a call for attention, for action, for nerve. Now the chords came crashing, followed by the running bridge of notes that led to chords of yet greater power, louder statement. And she played for Helga, poor Helga and her unknown fate. She played for all those imprisoned, tortured, and terrified. Chopin gave the means. Music made the statement—a universal, sweeping cry for freedom and the love of freedom. Nothing could quench that love of freedom. Nothing! Let the soldiers stand watch! Let them formulate their evil. Let them wait. In the end they would be vanquished.

There was that long moment's hiatus. Silence. Then applause came in a rush, a flood. The people roared. They clapped. They shouted "Bravo!" Julie's heart sang with her own strange joy and knowledge. *Not for me, not for me, but for Denmark, for freedom, for victory.*

◆ ◆ ◆

Afterward, everyone gathered at Julie's house—Cousin Boris, exuberant at his own cleverness, his son Michael, nodding and shaking Julie's hand, kissing her cheek. Of course Grandmother Sophie came with her friends. Aunt Bella and Uncle Aleksander beamed and told of other concerts, of the time they had been to Vienna, heard opera in Italy . . . "Ah my dears, those were the days," they said fondly. They praised Julie and kissed her and pinched her cheeks. Sasha had brought several of his friends from school. "Weren't you scared?" they said. "Are you on the concert stage?" they asked. "Can you play Scott Joplin?"

Julie offered them cakes and promised to play for them later—yes, she had Joplin and some other popular pieces, and they whooped with delight.

"My darling," her grandmother said, "you were wonderful. A pride to us all. You are growing up! A young lady already. I only wish to live long enough to see you under the *chuppah."*

Julie laughed. "I'm not planning to get married for quite a while, Grandmother. I am only fifteen."

"My mother was married at fourteen, and she bore six healthy children! And you—you have her looks, those beautiful dark eyes, that glowing skin."

Julie looked up to see Peter standing close by, smiling broadly. He gave her a look, a smile that made her feel flushed and indescribably happy.

He came to Julie when the first crush of congratulations had waned. She had gone to the kitchen to bring in a tray of small sandwiches.

"Congratulations, Julie," he said, standing in the doorway. "You were magnificent. I did not know you played."

"Do you play an instrument?" she asked, for the first time able to speak to Peter without feeling baffled or tongue-tied.

"No," he said. "But I like to sing. You know, they say in Palestine people are always singing. They sing while they dig and plant. We have been learning some of the songs."

"I know a few," Julie said. "Like 'Sholom Aleichem.'"

"Peace be to you," Peter translated. "It is both greeting and farewell."

Julie stood with the tray in her hands, looking at Peter, feeling not only the warmth of his words, but something else, something he wanted to say but could not. She wanted to ask him, "What is the matter?" But she hesitated, and in the silence he took a step closer.

"When you were done playing," he said, "I saw your tears."

"Music makes me feel very emotional," she said.

"I heard about your teacher."

Julie nodded, her throat suddenly feeling constricted.

"You played for her, didn't you?"

"Yes. For her, and for all the others." She took a deep breath, blinked the tears away. "I know what is happening," she said softly. "My parents and most of the Jews here don't want to talk about it. As if that will prevent it from coming here! All those laws the Nazis made in Germany, forbidding Jews to work, to marry, to travel. That yellow star! Did you know they have to wear a yellow star, as if they had to be tagged? Identified?"

"It can be a badge of honor," Peter said quietly. His face, suddenly, looked worn and tired.

"It is no honor to be singled out so that people can spit on you in the street!" she cried vehemently.

"You are right, Julie," Peter said quickly. "Do you know the story that is going around? About the king?"

She shook her head.

"That it was suggested that the Jews in Denmark should also be made to wear that yellow star. And the king is supposed to have said, if that is the case, he will be first person to wear one! And all the other Danes would follow him."

Julie chuckled. "I am sure the king feels that way, and most of the other people in Denmark, too. When they cheered so at the *allsang,* I know it was not for me. It was for all of us. For a free Denmark."

Peter gave her a long look. "Denmark is a lovely land, yes, like it says in the anthem. I wish . . ." He looked away. "Listen, Julie, sometimes people have to do things they themselves do not like. There are conflicts. Then we have to ask ourselves what is good not only for us, but for our people, the community. Judaism must survive. Jews must have a homeland. Some of us are needed to build it. Do you understand? We cannot just follow our own desires. Do you understand?"

She felt breathless and dazzled, more by his tone than by his words.

"Hello, you two! Are we ever going to get those sandwiches!" Julie's mother burst into the kitchen, her arms outstretched. "Come, Julie, you are the star of the afternoon. Everyone wants to see you!"

Friends and family quickly surrounded her.

"Julie, smile!" Niels stood back and snapped her picture, then pictures of her and Ingrid, Fredericka, and Peter. The photographs would preserve this wonderful day forever. But Julie also felt a strange sadness. Someday she would be looking at these pictures alone. Where would her friends be then? Might they all be scattered?

Some of us are needed . . . Peter's words rang back at her. Did he mean that she, too, should go to Palestine and become a pioneer, a builder? She loved this land where she was born. She could not imagine leaving Denmark, ever.

Chapter Thirteen

Niels

The world was changing. There was no news but war. Sirens shrieked out warning in the night as bombers flew over Copenhagen, aiming at German installations and factories. They were British planes. In their hearts the Danes wished them success, while at the same time they prayed that nobody would die in the raid. Niels and his family fled to the shelter, unless the planes seemed too far away to affect them. Then they gathered close in the living room by the potbellied stove to warm themselves, and they listened to the radio with its squeaky static, hoping for music or news from the front through the BBC. Even this was a secret thing, and yet Niels's father had no objection. The Germans had warned against listening to Allied broadcasts. The punishment would be severe. But the Danes longed for information as much as for food and warmth.

Fall turning to winter brought an icy cold to Copenhagen, quite unlike any cold Niels had ever known. The wind blew in great, freezing gusts. The trees, long having shed their leaves, seemed braced against it, frozen solid, and one wondered whether they would ever regain their bloom. People hurried along with their heads thrust down into their collars, with earmuffs and fur mittens, scarves and coats covering almost every inch of skin. They were bundled tight, like creatures buried inside a cocoon. The question was: Would they ever emerge? Would there be another spring?

Despite the cold, the king rode out every morning at ten, astride his magnificent black steed. People could set their clocks by the king's ride. There he was, wearing his uniform with the double row of brass buttons and his military cap. Niels and Fredericka and Ingrid went, with hundreds of others, to walk along the path of the royal promenade, then to stop and wave, smile, even to call out to this monarch, whose appearance meant they were still a people, still Danes.

As Niels stood looking up at the king, he gave a solemn salute, and his heart swelled with pride. He was working for the king as a secret emissary. Someday it might be told, but for now, it was enough that Niels knew. Meanwhile, it took every ounce of restraint to pretend he was only a schoolboy, uninterested in politics.

On the day the doctors from Bispebjerg Hospital were shot, his father came home looking more worn and gray than ever. The family first heard the news from a friend who called Niels's mother, hysterical, on the telephone. "Is Karl all right?" the woman had shrieked. "How do you know? Who would do such a thing? Killing doctors!"

Mother had telephoned the hospital immediately and was told, "Everything is fine. Do not worry, Kirsten. I am coming home now."

They waited for him, the entire family, nervous and upset. Father walked in and, like any other night, slowly took off his coat, put away his bag, sat down at the table. They all took their usual places, but tension filled the air like smoke.

"Tell us, Karl," Mother finally said.

"It is true. One of the nurses they took used to assist me. A fine woman." He reached for the platter of sandwiches, took several onto his plate. Niels saw how his hands trembled. Still, he began to eat.

"But why, Karl? To shoot doctors and nurses!"

"It was in retaliation for sabotage."

"But had these doctors done anything?"

"They were chosen at random. We have all been warned, Kirsten. These are dangerous times."

Niels watched his father, aghast, and he cried out, "*Platitudes!* You give us only platitudes. Of course it is dangerous, but how much more dangerous if they win!"

"Quiet, Niels," his mother shot back. "Don't dare to speak to your father in that tone!"

Fredericka sat rigid, fingering the small silver medallion around her neck. It was a gift from Peter, a replica of the Little Mermaid statue.

"In this house," Niels's father said sternly, "we will refrain from discussing politics. Is that clear?"

"Does that mean we can't talk about the occupation? About who rules, and what they do to people?" Niels asked brashly. "Does it include concentration camps?"

"Enough!" cried their father, slamming his hand down on the table. He rose, walking stiffly to the doorway. Then he turned and said, "There must be sanctuary somewhere. Home must be a place of peace." He gritted his teeth, looking at all of them, his longest gaze at Niels.

◆ ◆ ◆

Often Niels thought of the times when he and Emil were like brothers. Of course they used to argue, but their arguments had ended in friendship, with Emil's arm slung across Niels's shoulder. And they would both be grinning. Now they were like two warriors, and Niels felt isolated and angry.

The newspapers announced that some eight thousand young Danes had joined the German army on the eastern front to fight the Russians. Emil spoke of it, his eyes gleaming with pride and longing. "Don't you want to go into the fight?" he exclaimed. "I'm sick of sitting on the sidelines! We need to fight the Communists," he declared. "They terrorize people, send them to slave-labor camps."

"But aren't the Nazis the same?" Niels protested. "Haven't you heard about the things they do?"

"Zionist propaganda," Emil shot back. "Look, you need to educate yourself. Read the literature. Talk to some of the people who know."

"Like those guys you are hanging around with—they look like thugs!" Emil had taken to lounging at the school gates at noontime with a group of boys who held themselves apart, casting dark glances over their shoulders, spitting and smoking cigarettes.

"You mean Horace and Hans and Victor? They have strong ideas. They care about the shape the world is in. We're in a crisis, Niels."

"I agree with that," Niels snapped.

"We're fighting for our very survival."

"Whose survival?"

"Ours! White people, us! Don't you know that Jews control most of the money in the world? That they dominate elections?"

"That's absurd, Emil! There are so few Jews in Denmark, how could they control things?"

Emil snatched a Nazi newspaper, called *Kamptegnet.* "Look, it explains how the Jews tried to control everything in Germany. Look!"

Niels took the newspaper, his heart pounding with disbelief and anger. "Look," he cried, pointing, "it also says the Jews are like animals, inferior to Aryans. If that is so, how can so many of them be doctors and lawyers? How could they take over the entire country?"

"They are devious," Emil said. "That's how." He began to pace, stopping to glance at Niels, as if he were judging whether or not Niels could be trusted. "You know," he said, "what they really want is to take our women, to marry with them. Or more often, just have relations with them. Niels, they are polluting our race. Like those guys who said they came to Denmark just to learn farming. Those Zionists. What they really want is to take our women. To infiltrate our society. Like that fellow your sister hangs around with—that Jew."

"You mean Peter? What about him?"

"Why doesn't he stick to his own kind? What does he want with a decent Danish girl like Fredericka? He says he is going to go to Palestine—then why is he leading her on? Can't you see, he only wants to get her in bed."

"Shut up, Emil! I can't believe you would go this far, say these horrible things just out of jealousy."

"Don't be ridiculous!" Emil snapped. "This is politics. There is much more to this situation than you imagine. If you would come to some meetings—"

"Never!"

"—you would learn what is really going on."

◆ ◆ ◆

It was still strange and also exciting to go alone to that small apartment below the stairs, where Jens had sent him. Niels had made many trips by now. Always, there was that thrill of approaching danger.

Late one afternoon, Niels set out again, bundled against the cold, his fingertips numb inside his gloves. It was a good time to go, to get lost amid the crowds headed home after work. He would make it back home for dinner, with no questions to answer.

Going along the familiar streets, Niels kept his head low, turning now and then to be sure he was not being followed. He moved quickly, slid into the alley behind the buildings, pushed open a painted green door, splintered and scarred from use.

Niels entered the apartment, glancing about. It took several moments to grow accustomed to the fading light. There was a wooden worktable with two typewriters, a radio, and two primitive duplicating machines. The floor was cement, with a small scrap of old carpet that bunched up underneath the workers' feet. Three straight chairs stood empty, for the workers were continually moving or fast asleep from exhaustion.

Now a man leaned over a wooden worktable, correcting copy. Another pecked at a typewriter. The man at the typewriter gave Niels a slight nod. Niels murmured a greeting. Uncle Jens had warned him, "Keep talk to a minimum. If you are caught . . . the less you know, the better."

A woman with stiff gray hair worked at one of the copiers, reinking the gelatin pad, pressing down papers one by one. Crumpled, spoiled papers littered the floor. Even the "good" copies were often smudged and wrinkled. But it was the message that counted:

NAZI THUGS ATTACK SYNAGOGUE

In the dead of night, as cowards do, they came with torches and gasoline, attempting to set the synagogue ablaze. In Germany, hundreds of synagogues have been destroyed. As if faith can be obliterated by fire!

From now on, the synagogue will have its own early-fire-detection system, wired directly to the Danish police. Naturally, our German occupation forces were not at first eager to approve such a plan. But leaders of the Jewish community along with Danish ministers finally negotiated this result.

Other articles praised the brave freedom fighters who crept out at night to disarm German motor vehicles or to blow up a bridge where German trucks were moving out Danish goods. Another item mentioned more subtle tactics, like influencing factory workers to slow production down to a crawl. Frustrate the Germans! Let them wait month after month for promised supplies. And when finally the goods arrived, time and again they were defective, with faulty wiring, mismatched parts—and a Danish worker laughing up his sleeve.

The room was freezing cold. A lanky teenage boy lay fast asleep on the floor, under the assembly table. They had obviously worked all night getting out the papers. Stacks of finished papers were lying about; empty bottles and sticky plates spoke of meals hastily consumed, refuse hardly discarded before the work had to go on.

The boy stretched and sat up, running his hand through a

mass of curly red hair. "Hello," he said. "Who are you?"

"Just call me Stork," Niels said with a responding grin. "I deliver. How about you? I haven't seen you here before."

The boy got up and extended his hand. "Call me Jacob. After one of the Hebrew patriarchs." Standing at full height, he looked older and more serious.

"You are a Hebrew?"

"I am many things." He groaned and scratched himself vigorously across both shoulders. "How did you get here?"

"Oh, I followed a breadcrumb trail," Niels said evasively. "And you?"

"Broke my arm. Got mixed up with some rowdies at a demonstration. Of course, I had nothing to do with it," he said with a smirk. "So I met some people at the clinic, and here I am." He slumped down on one of the chairs, pulled out another for Niels, who remained standing.

A tall, thin girl came in, wearing a shabby black sweater with the sleeves pushed up, a thick maroon muffler, and a gray skirt. Everything about her looked worn, her long hair, drooping eyes, and skinny legs. But when she smiled, suddenly a new energy came into the crowded, ugly room. "Hello! I am Lisbeth, Jacob's friend. You? I heard you are the Stork. A wonderful name. Now there are three of us. Come on! Let's have some refreshment."

She went to a small hot plate where a bent old coffeepot stood. She licked her finger, touched it to the side of the pot, and nodded. "Witch's piss," she said, "but at least it's hot. What do we have to eat?" She half turned toward Jacob. "Anything at all?"

"Some pretzels. There's a jar of old herring and some mustard . . ." Jacob pointed to a shelf.

"Perfect! Mustard and pretzels—come on, Stork. We have to talk. We have to make plans." Her features and her hands expressed action, excitement. Her eyes were suddenly alive and bright. "How many papers are you taking? Can you use five hundred? A thousand? We will make more. Where will you take them?"

"I—maybe to the railroad station."

"Perfect! Now, that's using your head. You can leave them in compartments, on benches at the station, even in the newspaper stand—how about that?"

"I thought I would take some to the shipyards and factories. You know, to boost morale, get the workers on our side."

"Excellent, perfect!" Lisbeth cried. She grinned at Jacob. "He's all right."

Jacob gave her a weary glance. "You are too trusting."

"I trust nobody but you—and Stork. Look at his face! Such a face you have to trust."

Jacob got up, went over to the man at the typewriter. They conferred briefly. The man glanced over at Niels and nodded.

Lisbeth said, "We were working all night until noon today. Five in the morning, somebody knocked at the door. We did not move or even breathe, and they just left. If the Germans had come in here and seen this"—she waved at the illegal papers—"we would have been done for. But," she said with a smile, "here we are. They are stupid!"

Jacob returned and muttered to Lisbeth, "You talk too much." He nodded toward Niels. "He's all right. Three is enough, though. Don't take on anyone else."

Niels felt his head spinning—what were they talking about? He glanced from one to the other, saw their approval. Three musketeers, he thought.

Jacob stood before him now, inquiring, "What else have you done? Anything interesting?"

Niels shook his head, pressed his lips tight. This could be a test.

Jens had told him, "You must keep everything in your head. And don't talk. *Don't talk.* Remember."

Suddenly Jacob grabbed Niels by the arm, pressing hard on his biceps.

"Strong enough," he muttered.

"For what?" Niels asked.

"I will tell you when the time comes," said Jacob. "Can you get out at night?"

"Yes." His heart began to race. *Yes, yes!*

Chapter Fourteen

Fredericka's Diary

Peter is gone. I was so worried!

I feel dry, empty of words. Maybe it is from crying.

When I found out he was gone, I could not believe it. It cannot be true, I thought, because he would have told me! He knows he could trust me with anything, everything. If he had to leave, why wouldn't he come to me to say good-bye? So it is obvious. He did not trust me. Or he was afraid to tell me. I thought he was brave and good. Now I see that he is a coward.

No, I do not mean that.

Tears bleed out all the sense in a person's mind. Tears drain all the energy out of one's body. I feel dried up and exhausted. I will never laugh again. Mother says she understands. How can she? She tells me stories about her youth and about friends who had such and such an experience, and how they wept and how they grieved and now they can be happy again. Who cares? What difference does it make?

If I knew where he was, when he left, and exactly how and why, I could tolerate it. Because then there would be something to explain to myself. Now there is only emptiness.

He sent his friend Dov with a message. It was not even in

writing. Dov came and knocked on the door last Sunday afternoon, and he stood there like a messenger from the telegraph company, eyes straight ahead and shoulders squared, like a soldier. He did not look at me, and when he said the words, it was as if they spilled out of his mouth one by one, like meaningless objects in which he had no interest. I will never forget the words. I heard them only once, but immediately they became burned into my mind. He said: "Peter sent me to tell you that he has left Denmark. He wanted you to know. He did not want you to be angry or to be left with uncertainty. These are difficult times. Peter could not tell you facts of his departure. It would endanger others. Peter said he will never forget you. He wishes the times were different."

The first words that sprang to my lips were, "You lie!"

Poor Dov, he went quite pale and shook his head and began again. "Peter sent me to tell you . . ."

I began to tremble all over. I remember standing there, feeling the shaking in my hands and knees, wanting to control it, but I could not make it stop. I have never trembled that way. It was as if a sickness suddenly swept over my entire body, moving from the inside out to my hands and legs. All I could do was try to catch my breath, to think, but thoughts kept on circling around those words.

At last I think I whispered, "Did he say anything else?" Only one word, then, was in my heart. Only that one word. And I remember thinking, if he said it, if he said that one word, then everything else would be all right. Then I would stop trembling. Then I could feel whole again.

But Dov shook his head and said, "No. That was all."

CHAPTER FIFTEEN

Julie

Julie's mother lay in bed with a high fever. Julie heard her coughing and moaning from across the hallway. She called, "How are you, Mama?"

"I'm all right," came the weak reply. "Don't come in here. It could be contagious."

Mrs. Giesler took Sammy to her house. He went happily, for Mrs. Giesler's three grown sons had taught him to play cards and dice. That evening Sammy telephoned, thrilled at having won ten kroner from his hosts.

Father, who was staying home to take care of things, admonished Sammy. "Be a good boy. Mind Mrs. Giesler. And remember, don't draw on a full house."

It was a rare moment of laughter. Julie's father, frightened by sickness, and lonely, crept through the house on tiptoe. "I have sent for Dr. Nelson," he told Julie. "He's coming later tonight, when he gets home from the hospital." He came into Julie's room and pulled up a chair beside her desk. "I'm worried about your mother. She is not very strong. Things affect her, Julie, in a personal way. The occupation, the worry—it eats at her."

"But she has her work," said Julie. "The library keeps her engrossed."

"It exhausts her. I ask her to rest, but does she listen? When Sammy was born—right before, when the ambulance came—"

"I remember, Papa. It was a terrible day."

"She was so sick. I'm not sure she ever completely recovered. Julie." He paused. "Promise me you will look after Sammy. The two of you must stick together."

"But we have Mrs. Giesler, Far. What do you mean?" Her father's face was so serious, forehead creased. The lines around his mouth made him look old and sad. And she knew, suddenly, what he meant. Later, when she and Sammy were grown up, even if they were married and had children of their own, they must still stick together. They were family.

"I love Sammy, Papa," she said ardently. "I will always love him. He is my brother."

Later, Ingrid's father, Dr. Nelson, came over and spoke softly to Julie and her father. "Be sure Edith stays in bed," he said. "I'm going to prescribe some medicine for her. Actually, the Germans requisition most of the drugs we have. There is a great shortage of medicine, as with everything. I have five of them on morphine at this moment, and several on sulfur."

"You mean, you also treat the Germans?" Julie exclaimed.

"Of course, Julie. We treat anybody who is ill."

"But—but they killed doctors and nurses! And for no reason."

Dr. Nelson shook his head. "Sometimes the reasons are irrational and evil—but reasons everyone has aplenty. The Germans want two things from us, respect and fear. If they cannot get the first, they will at least get the second."

"But still you go to the hospital every day."

"I am not afraid of them," Dr. Nelson said, wrapping up his

stethoscope and dropping it into his bag. "Actually, they get thugs to do their dirty work, so it is all 'unofficial.' Our ministers, then, cannot accuse the Germans of breaking their bargain to keep the status quo. No, they send hooligans to commit murder. But it has nothing to do with us, Julie."

She felt hot, smoldering. *Nothing to do with us? It has everything to do with us!* But she did not speak.

Far placed his hand on Dr. Nelson's arm. "Karl, tell me. What is wrong with her? Will she . . ."

"Your wife needs bed rest, Philip. Don't look so glum—that expression is enough to make anyone sick! Seriously, just keep her quiet and give her the medicine."

"What medicine?"

"Digoxin," replied Dr. Neson. "In common parlance, foxglove, a folk remedy. We use it when the heart is affected."

"The heart!" Julie exclaimed. "I thought she has the flu."

"Sometimes the virus settles in the heart. It can leave a person with residual damage and weakness. She will need extra rest and all the help you can give her."

"Of course." Julie felt a gathering of sorrow, almost despair. Last year Madelaine, a girl in her class, lost her mother to a heart attack. Everyone pitied Madelaine, but nobody knew what to say to her. Because death was so remote and improbable, and yet there it was, close by.

Never had she felt so alone. Later, when Ingrid called, wanting to come over, Julie rushed to meet her, despite the icy cold. They met halfway and ran back to Julie's house.

In Julie's room, Ingrid sank down on the carpet and pulled Julie down beside her, whispering, "I have to tell you something. I read Fredericka's diary."

"You didn't!" Julie gasped.

"Peter left. He never even said good-bye. She is heartbroken. She cries in the night. She thinks I am asleep, but I can hear her crying."

"How awful! What does she say?"

"She refuses to talk about it. That's why I read her diary. I had to know. She is my sister, after all. And now Emil is hanging around all the time, telling her what a terrific writer she is. You know he has always had a crush on her. Emil says he knows someone who publishes a newspaper. He wants Fredericka to submit some of her poems and to write articles. He took her ice skating the other day."

"So, I guess that's good," Julie said. "Then she can get over her heartbreak about Peter." Her heart pounded as she thought of their last conversation: *Sometimes people have to do things they themselves do not like . . . we cannot just follow our own desires.* Where could he be? It was nearly impossible, she had heard, for people to get to Palestine. Some Jews managed to go to London or to Sweden. But why wouldn't Peter have at least explained his plans?

"Poor Fredericka," Julie said. "Had she and Peter talked about getting . . ." She could not bring herself to say the word.

"She wanted to go with him," Ingrid said, "wherever he went. She would have gone with him to Palestine. She saw herself like Karen Blixen, following the man she loved." Ingrid leaned back against the bed, arms crossed, hugging herself. "Isn't it romantic? Isn't it beautiful?"

Julie whispered, "Is pain beautiful?"

"'Better to have loved and lost,'" Ingrid quoted, "'than never to have loved at all.'"

"Have you been in love?" Julie asked. "Really in love?"

Ingrid frowned. "I don't know. That day in the park last

summer, when Lars and I were in the canoe, and he rowed into the glade and kissed me—I felt something. Was it love? I don't know. I liked it, though. I liked the kiss. It was very warm and very—um—personal."

They both laughed. "I guess it would be," mused Julie.

She had, for many nights, lain awake imagining the touch of Peter's lips on hers. She counted the times they had all been together. There was that first Seder, the evening at Tivoli, some trips to the shore, excursions to the docks and the museum. It was always a group, sitting together at Ny Haven or in the park, having fruit juice and pretzels or ice cream, joking and talking. Peter stood out. She had memorized his smile, his expressions, the way he moved. She felt oddly dizzy. She sighed.

"You're in love with him," Ingrid suddenly said.

Julie started. "No! How absurd."

"Yes; yes, you are. I've seen it from the beginning. That very first night he came to your house for the Seder. You couldn't take your eyes off him. You kept track of every time he and Fredericka were together. You tried to be subtle, but you were always asking me about Fredericka and him. And the way you looked at him. Only Fredericka didn't see it. I'm glad Fredericka never knew."

"Me, too," Julie said in a muffled tone. She sat, staring down at the carpet. Suddenly she felt freezing cold and pulled the feather quilt from her bed, wrapping it around her shoulders, covering Ingrid, too. She hadn't meant to cry, but the tears came nevertheless, and the two of them sat under the quilt together, and Ingrid whispered, "Oh, Julie, dear, please, please don't cry."

◆ ◆ ◆

With the advent of spring, warmer weather, and brightness in the air, Julie expected her mother to improve. But the virus had attacked her heart, leaving her weak and listless. She got up each morning as before and dragged herself to work, returning earlier than usual, looking pale and tired.

Julie took it upon herself to prepare dinner every night and to shop for the necessary items each afternoon. It brought her closer, somehow, to the reality of men and women living their daily lives under a shadow. In the shops, in secret publications that she found slipped into her grocery bag or into her hand in passing, information came. Leaflets and newspapers began to appear at the door, sometimes with the morning milk delivery or simply pushed into their mail slot. At night Mother turned on the radio, and Julie sat beside her on the floor, listening to reports about the war. Then she and her mother talked about the latest campaign, German gains or losses, Allied troop movements or sabotage. Sabotage was a constant theme.

"Did you hear," her mother asked one night, "about those teenagers who were arrested?"

"I saw a flyer," Julie replied. "I only glanced at it."

"Mere children!" her mother cried. She coughed, holding her hands to her chest, wheezing. "My—my medicine." She groped for the pills, swallowed them with water. "None older than seventeen—the Germans arrested them as saboteurs."

"What will happen to them? Will they be shot?"

Her mother was seized with coughing. Far, looking in, pointed to the door. "You are upsetting your mother with all this talk," he said sternly. "Go and let her rest, Julie. Go on, don't you have some homework to do?"

Julie went into the kitchen. In her backpack she had saved several of the illegal papers. Now she spread them out on the table. There was a photograph of seven boys and girls, young, with solemn faces. They called themselves the Churchill Club. Each one was tagged, like a criminal, with a number. They had stolen weapons, set fires, blown up railroad tracks. One of them made a statement: "If the adults refuse to do anything, we have to take it upon ourselves."

Julie felt her eyes stinging. She knew she could never be a hero. There was no telling what would happen to these young saboteurs. They could be tortured. How would they endure it? Perhaps they were given cyanide pills to take in case of capture. Julie had heard about that. She pushed the paper away, about to crumple it into a ball. Instead, she flattened out the page and stared at the faces of the young freedom fighters, knowing that she and they were eons apart.

◆ ◆ ◆

Poor Sammy had to spend his fourth birthday in an air-raid shelter. Julie organized the children, singing songs and passing out hard candies. She told stories, all the Hans Christian Andersen fairy tales she remembered.

"It is not so terrible," her mother said, though she coughed and shivered in the dampness. Julie laid a blanket around her mother's shoulders. "Think of the poor people in other countries. London has not had a quiet night in years. The people's nerves must be shot."

Her mother's hands, Julie noticed, trembled, and her voice was always rough and rasping, as if she had a constant cold. She cleared her throat, sucked lozenges, drank cup after cup of hot tea. Still, the hoarseness remained.

One Sunday a driving rain and gusty wind whistled through the house, yet Julie's mother prepared to go out, pulling her cape and boots from the hall closet.

"Where on earth do you think you are going?" Father demanded.

"It is," Mother gasped, "Aunt Monica's birthday. Ninety-two today. I always"—she coughed, cleared her throat—"bring her something. She is expecting—"

"Nonsense! You are not going out in this weather."

"Don't dictate to me, Philip! She is my *aunt.* I am not going to let her think her birthday means so little . . ."

"Julie." She caught her father's pleading look.

"I'll go," Julie said, reaching for the cape and umbrella. "I don't mind."

"It is too windy to bicycle," her mother objected, "and the bus line—"

"I can walk," Julie said. "Look, I will take Far's big umbrella. I won't even get wet. Do we have a present for Aunt Monica?"

"Some bath salts," her mother said, "and a lovely cologne . . . oh, Julie, are you sure?"

"Doesn't she like those chocolate pastilles? I could buy some on the way."

"You're an angel."

Julie made a face, lips thrust out, eyes crossed.

"Go on—if the wind blows, your face will stick that way!"

Julie gathered the gifts in an oilcloth bag. "I feel like Red Riding Hood," she said, wrapping a red woolen scarf around her head.

"Don't talk to any wolves," teased her mother.

"Don't talk to *anyone,*" admonished Far.

"I want to come, too!" Sammy called.

"No. It's too wet. Mama needs you to play games with her, don't you, Mama? I'll try to bring you some chocolates. I can't promise, you know."

"I know," Sammy said, his brow wrinkled. "We are at war. And the soldiers are eating all the chocolate."

The streets were slick and dark, the sky a misty gray. Wetness whipped into Julie's face, pulling the umbrella down, so that she had to close it before she could continue. She walked rapidly, trying to avoid dripping eaves and awnings. Within minutes her woolen shawl was soaked. She pulled it off and tucked it under her arm.

Rain in her hair felt curiously free, almost refreshing. She had heard that some movie stars washed their hair in rainwater to make it shine. If it worked, she would tell Ingrid.

The chocolate shop was barred and dark, with a sign in the window. CLOSED DUE TO SHORTAGES.

Poor Aunt Monica would have to do without her pastilles. This might be her last chance at ninety-two. Poor Aunt Monica. Pity almost overcame Julie's repugnance. The Home for the Aged was not one of her favorite places.

A bleak feeling came over Julie, and as if to match her mood, the sky became darker. The streets had emptied out; people fled from the worsening storm. Julie hurried on, breathing hard as she battled wind and fog.

Voices reached her first, breaking through the mist, that unmistakable quality of foreign speech. Then she heard the raucous laughter.

"Ah, look! A pretty one. And she is all alone."

Julie's knowledge of German, after three years of instruction at school, was still imperfect, but she understood not only the words but the laughter that followed.

"Doesn't look like a Dane."

"Looks like one of those Jews."

"No—Jews have big noses."

"She looks just right for you, Willi!"

"You must be crazy, Oscar."

The soldiers stood straight in front of her. Julie's heart hammered, her throat grew dry. She glanced about—nothing, nobody to help her. The shops were closed, all except for an inn nearly a block away. If she tried to run, would they follow? Would it be great sport for them to catch her? And then . . . ?

There were three of them, looking at her with bold eyes, laughing now at her discomfort. She felt their closeness, felt the shiver across her spine.

Just walk away, she told herself. Say nothing, don't meet their eyes. She took a step or two.

"You!" the one called Willi shouted. His Danish was flawed, but adequate. "Girl! We want to talk to you. Come here."

Julie froze. And now all her senses seemed sharpened. She felt an odd vibration through the soles of her feet, heard a distant sound. *Clang! Clang!*

"You! Come here!"

Julie heard the rumble, saw the flash of a spark as the car's electric pole moved across the cable.

Now! The next moment Julie was racing toward the streetcar, running madly. She skidded on the damp cobblestones, lurched and nearly fell, regained her balance, ran on while behind her she heard the shouts of the soldiers. As the streetcar slowed in a wide ark, Julie leaped onto the platform. She stood, clutching the bar, panting, looking straight ahead, fighting back tears.

"Good show, miss," someone murmured. It was a man wearing an overcoat and leather gloves, standing beside her on the platform. As the car gained speed, he lifted his hat in a mild salute. The conductor stopped to glance at her bus card and give her a nod and a smile.

It took several minutes for Julie to feel calm again. Then she realized she was headed in the wrong direction. When she got off, she turned, getting her bearings. Resolutely, Julie set out for the Home for the Aged. At last she approached the high iron gate surrounding the complex. She hurried past the synagogue with its massive stone walls, through the large courtyard, to the narrow door of the Home. Immediately she was flooded with smells of antiseptic, boiling cabbage, and a heavy odor of humanity too long closed in without sunshine and open space. The walls were painted a yellow green, oddly streaked with patches of white, where perhaps mold had begun and repairs were undertaken. Linoleum on the floor, a spidery pattern of gray and black, curled up at the edges.

Julie walked cautiously to the doorway that led to the "day-room," from which came sounds of life, a distant buzzing from a radio, murmurs, someone tapping a spoon against a tabletop. The table filled the room almost completely. At various angles stood a plethora of chairs, each one different—wood or metal, with seats of straw, cane, or imitation leather. It seemed that anyone in the city who had an old chair to spare brought it here—a balm to the conscience, perhaps. For it was clear that in this Home there could never be enough attention or love, simply because it was not really home.

"Hello!" Julie called out, making her voice bright. "Hello, hello!"

Three men turned. One called back, "Good day, miss!" The other two smiled, one with perfect false teeth, the other almost toothless. The man who had been tapping his spoon stopped abruptly, rose to his feet, and pulled out a chair. "Have a seat, young lady!" His perfect teeth gleamed at her; he must have been quite a dandy once, she thought.

"I've come to see my great-aunt Monica. Is she here?" Silly question—where else would she be?

A male nurse in a white tunic came in, rubbing his hands together. "Yes, yes, we will bring her out, of course. Monica, my dear, you have a visitor!" he piped. He turned back to Julie. "Her birthday today! Ninety-two. We made a cake. Saved flour for weeks. White frosting—can't get chocolate."

"That's nice," said Julie.

The men were talking loudly, waving their hands, adjusting the small *kippot* on their heads. Several women came in, intent on selecting their chairs.

"Did you hear?" asked one woman, wearing a pink turban. "The Germans forced Minister Moller to resign."

"They have a noose around our necks," said the toothless man. "Hitler, *v'mach she'mom*, flew into a rage because King Christian only answered his birthday telegram with two words. 'Many thanks! Christian Rex.' Ha!"

"So now he will take it out on the Jews," said a blond woman. "It is always so."

"Already they want to enact special laws against us."

"The Danes won't allow it."

"What can they do if the Nazis get serious? If they bring more troops? Do you know this new commandant, Werner Best, *v'mach she'mom*—may his name be blotted out! He is a poisonous anti-Semite—he wrote articles recommending concentration camps."

"Politics, always politics," complained one of the women. She wore a long, flowered dressing gown. "We are having chicken for lunch," she told Julie. "Do you like chicken?"

"Yes, I do." She had not imagined eating here. The woman went to the cupboard and brought out a stack of paper plates.

Another set out the silverware and paper cups. The room began to fill with people and all the preparations of a party. Suddenly it seemed like any room, any place where people gather for fun.

"Julie! My dear," Aunt Monica called as her wheelchair came through the doorway. She grasped her cane, pushing herself upright, reaching out. Julie went to her, offered her arm. "How lovely to see you! How is your dear mama?"

"A bit under the weather, Aunt Monica," said Julie. "Happy birthday! I tried to get pastilles for you, but—"

"Do not worry, Julie. Seeing you is present enough. What? You also brought . . . ah, how lovely. I do love cologne! Your mother is an angel. I shall write her a note."

Soon every chair was taken and more were brought in by the aides. Platters of chicken, vegetables, and mashed potatoes were set out, and everyone ate with gusto. "Delicious," Julie said, biting into a crispy chicken leg.

"Yes, the food is very good," said Aunt Monica, wiping her lips. "Kosher, of course." Then came the cake, decorated with candles, and somebody suggested a song.

"Does anybody play?"

Now Julie noticed the ancient upright piano in a shadowy corner, under the window. "I do."

"Play for us! Oh, yes, do!"

Julie made her way to the piano, lifted the lid, and viewed the keys, chipped and discolored with age. Like the people, she thought with a heavy feeling. Everything is old and worn-out. She was filled with an inexplicable sadness. But she glanced at Aunt Monica, who waved her hand from across the room and lifted her teacup in a toast. *"L'chaim!"* she called. "To life!"

Julie pulled over a small round stool, sat down, and ran her index finger across the keys in a swift, brilliant run of notes that proclaimed, "Listen! It's time!"

Then she played a merry polka, feeling the rhythm through her hands, her entire body. Someone began to clap. Feet tapped. The tabletop became a drum. "Ho! Ho!" A few of the men sang along, "Ta-da-dum-dum, ta-da-dup-dup!" They were loving it, coming alive. "Again! Play it again!"

Once again Julie played the polka, then a mazurka by Chopin, some dances of Schubert, a Viennese waltz, and then the old, familiar songs that everyone knew. As she played, warmth came into her body. Her face felt flushed and damp, her fingers clever and swift. In her heart she sang along with the old people, chorus after chorus, and she thought to herself, laughing silently, So it was for this that I have studied piano these past seven years! Just for this day!

"Happy birthday!" she called out at last. Everyone sang for Aunt Monica, and later, they kissed Julie's cheeks and pressed her hands and sent her home, glowing.

Chapter Sixteen

Niels

Jacob knew something about everything. He was eighteen, had been out of school for two years already, entirely on his own. He and Lisbeth had met in Poland following a Nazi raid. "Everyone in my village was rounded up," Jacob said. He told the story matter-of-factly, without emotion. "I heard the trucks coming. It was thick night, black as anything. My father and mother were downstairs when the soldiers came pounding on the door. I slept in a little attic room, with a window leading to the roof. I used to go up there as a small boy and look up at the stars. I went out to the roof and jumped down at the lowest pitch, onto the garden. I landed on a compost pile! What a mess!"

"We met in the forest," added Lisbeth. "I also ran away, but not from home. My parents had already been arrested, and I was in a convent. The sisters were good to me, but"—she shrugged—"most of the children were very young. I felt so confined! I knew there were people in the forest, hiding out, resistance people . . . I wanted to be active."

Jacob, with a wave of his hand and a grin, said, "When I was in the forest, a patrol came. I jumped into a ditch, but—"

"I was there first," said Lisbeth, laughing. "He landed on top of me. Nearly broke my back!"

"How did you get to Denmark?" Niels asked, looking from one to the other. Somehow they seemed like identical twins, finishing each other's sentences. The expressions in their eyes were the same, deep and haunted, but suddenly shining with life.

"Walked," they said together, then burst out laughing. "Until we got to the sea," added Lisbeth. "Then we went by boat, straight to Copenhagen." She shrugged in her usual way. "I had some jewelry. It served to pay for our passage. Now," she said with a laugh, "he owes me."

"How come you speak Danish?"

Lisbeth said, "We are still learning, but it's not so difficult."

"Not when you already speak four other languages," Jacob put in.

"Why did you choose Denmark?" Niels wanted to know.

"Denmark chose us," said Jacob.

"We were headed for London, but when we got to Copenhagen—"

"It is a beautiful city," Jacob said. "Next, I want to see San Francisco."

"San Francisco!" Niels exclaimed, looking from Jacob to Lisbeth.

"We want to see the world," she said, nodding. "All those gangsters . . ."

"Dillinger, Al Capone . . . they have gunfights in the streets, don't you know?"

Niels laughed. "That is only in the movies."

Jacob suddenly became serious. "We have a job to do tomorrow morning. Do you want to come with us?"

"Of course! What is it?"

"Lessons," said Lisbeth. "We are teaching lessons."

"To a *stikker,"* added Jacob. "In tight with the Nazi police. Informer."

"Where does he live?"

"In an apartment building, third floor."

"What needs to be done?" Niels kept his face blank, hiding his excitement. "What happens to a *stikker?"*

They both smiled. Jacob brushed an imaginary speck from his sleeve. He pursed his lips, in obvious imitation of an American gangster. "You will see."

"Meanwhile," Niels said, "I can make some more deliveries." He took up an armful of papers, glancing at the headlines. PIONEER YOUTH DISCOVERED . . . CROSSING THE BORDER INTO BAVARIA . . . BOUND FOR PALESTINE . . . ARRESTED . . .

"What's this?" His heart beat fiercely as he sank down with the paper, his eyes scanning the text. He looked up at Lisbeth and Jacob.

"What do you know about this?" Jacob asked.

"You're white as chalk," said Lisbeth.

"I—we know somebody . . . a *halutz* student." The word felt odd in his mouth. Niels had never said it before. It suddenly cast him into an alliance with Peter, with Fredericka, who walked around in ghostly silences, staring into space.

"They have been trying to get out of Denmark," Lisbeth said.

"To Sweden?" Niels asked. He had heard about Jews leaving for Sweden; it was a tricky business. Sweden was supposed to be neutral. He didn't imagine the Germans liked to have their prey escaping to Sweden.

"No. They were determined to make it through the Balkans to Turkey, then to Palestine. Some of the boys . . ." Jacob glanced about. "I suppose I can tell you now. The plan has failed, and they will not try it again. Too many have been . . ."

"Lost," Lisbeth supplied. "They found a very clever way, but . . ."

"Very dangerous," Jacob put in. "Foolish, perhaps, suicidal, but some did make it."

"How? What?" Niels gasped, needing to know.

"Well, they discovered that there is space underneath a railroad car for a person to lie flat, between the wheels and the bottom of the car. Very dangerous, of course. A couple of the boys actually made it, got to Germany, and came back again to tell the others it could be done. But then five boys lost their lives trying. A couple of others were caught in Hamburg, Germany. We don't know what happened to them, whether they were executed or sent to concentration camps."

A hundred questions went through Niels's mind. His throat felt parched, his body heavy. He wished he had not heard this. How could he keep it from Fredericka?

"Do you have their names?" he asked at last.

"No names. But they have all disbanded."

"How do you know all this?"

"We have ways. We have our own *stikkers,* too."

"Just one more thing," Niels said, his heart racing. "How were they caught? Was it an informer?"

Jacob shrugged. "Who can say? I think they probably got exhausted, probably ran out of food and water, lying under that horrible train. It could have made them careless. Or someone saw them. The Germans keep dogs to sniff out impostors. Can you imagine lying flat on your back without moving for two days and nights? And with the noise of that train above you?"

"No."

"Tomorrow morning, then," Jacob said.

"Meet us here," Lisbeth added. "Nine o'clock. Can you get out of school?"

"If you can get out of Poland," he retorted, "I can get out of school."

◆ ◆ ◆

He was early. All night the thought of something big had churned in his mind. Whatever it was, he was ready. To be with Jacob and Lisbeth meant more than going out alone with a sack of sugar to disable a truck, or even with matches and gasoline. Three in a war makes it real, he thought. Besides, he liked them. He had never before felt such a bond with people so different from himself. Everything about them was paradoxically strange but comfortable—the way they moved, the things they talked about, their intense seriousness interspersed with sudden laughter. They had done things in Poland; Niels did not know exactly what, but he could sense they were risky, even reckless acts of violence against the Nazis. Heroes, he thought. They are heroes, and they don't even know it.

He saw them coming, Lisbeth with her arms swinging, she and Jacob walking with long strides, coming past him without any sign of recognition, except for a slight curling of Jacob's fingers as they passed.

Niels paused, then began to saunter behind them, circling around several buildings, turning back a few times, until they arrived at a large three-story apartment house, a chaste graystone front and barred windows below.

Jacob led the way inside, up a flight of dark, narrow stairs. Lisbeth turned, smiled at Niels, and motioned for him to follow. A few sounds, rumblings, a baby's thin cry, came from behind doors. Someone was listening to music from the radio. The song was a rousing German combat refrain: *"We are marching on to England . . . we will conquer England!"*

Niels shuddered against the singing; he hated those constant songs, joy over conquest, the beauty of Germany, sweet homeland, Germany above all! The alien songs stuck in his head, and he could not dislodge them.

They had reached the top of the third floor. Jacob craned his neck, then motioned for Niels and Lisbeth to follow along the narrow, dark hallway. Odors of cookery and urine, old wood and wax combined into an overwhelming stench. Niels held his breath as they made their way to the last apartment on the left. The heavy door was shut.

"He's gone to work," Jacob whispered.

"How do you know?" Niels whispered back.

"It's obvious. No light through the cracks, no morning paper."

"Come on," said Lisbeth. "As soon as I open it . . ." She took a long wire from her bag, inserted it into the lock. With her head tilted to one side and bent down so that her ear was close to the lock, she manipulated the wire back and forth until suddenly she gave the door a shove with the flat of her hand. It popped open. Swiftly she pulled Jacob inside. Niels followed.

They stood in the silent room surveying the apartment with its narrow settee, a drop-leaf table and two chairs, an old commode, and a wooden sea chest. In the tiny kitchen stood a two-burner stove and open shelves filled with mismatching crockery, a few pots and utensils, a few staples, and a jar of coins. The bedroom had only a bed and a chair and several cardboard boxes upon which clothes were piled—underwear, pants, a heavy sweater, and shirts.

It felt peculiar and wrong to be lurking in another person's private domain. Niels shuddered. He glanced at Jacob. "What are we waiting for?" Jacob said in a robust tone. "Come on! This is how we inform informers that we do not want them among us!"

Lisbeth threw open the window. Laughing, she and Jacob ran to the bedroom, swept all the clothing off the shelf in one motion, ran to the window, and let it fly. Niels stood dumbfounded, watching. "Quick!" Lisbeth called out. "I'll get the utensils. You boys do the heavy stuff." She took an armful of dishes from the cupboard and sent them crashing down.

Niels hung back. "What if somebody hears all this racket? What if they report us?"

Jacob pulled his arm. "Nobody cares," he retorted. "People don't want to get involved. Don't you know that?"

"Still—they might call the police."

"They won't," Jacob said. "We'll be quick. Come on! Be strong." He ran into the living room, grasped the sofa. "Help me, Stork. Up—easy—let it go! Lucky the apartment faces the back and not the street. See how perfect this is? We have a guardian angel helping us!"

The sofa crashed down on top of the clothes, the dishes and pots, followed by the table, which broke into a dozen pieces. Chairs made a robust crackling sound. The sideboard first wedged itself into the windowsill and then soared down to join the other offerings.

Someone below hollered out a window, "What bloody business is this? What are you doing?"

"Only the king's work!" shouted back Lisbeth, retreating and overcome with giggles.

A strange sense of exhilaration gripped Niels, replacing all thoughts of what he was doing here, of lawlessness, crime, or retribution. Now, as he surveyed the heaps below, he was infused with a great sense of power and rightness. He glanced at his watch. Only five minutes had passed, but this surge of action had powered him up, expanded all his senses. He half expected sirens and flames to burst up from below, surrounded by cheering crowds.

Jacob pulled him roughly by the arm. "Come on. That's all. We're going."

They hurried silently down a flight of back stairs. The small door opened onto a side yard where trash cans were stored. Several rusted-out appliances crowded the gate. Niels stepped over a jagged piece of metal. It caught on his trouser leg, ripping the fabric, gashing his flesh.

Jacob and Lisbeth leaped out onto the street and began walking away. Niels limped after them. He felt the blood running down his leg, into his shoe. Lisbeth stopped at a bus bench. Niels flung himself down beside her. She gave him a handkerchief. "Tie this around," she said softly.

Jacob sat down, his arm around Lisbeth. He put back his head and began to laugh. He laughed so heartily that several passersby had to stop and smile, nodding over the joke they did not know but could somehow appreciate.

"Wait until that fellow comes home tonight!" Jacob slapped his thigh. "Oh, I would love to see his face!"

"But—how did you know about him?" Niels asked. He wound the handkerchief around his leg, pressed against the gash with the flat of his hand.

"Good source. Unimpeachable. A Danish policeman lives in the building. He has a small room. He has been watching the place. He can tell who is a thug and a *stikker;* it just takes a little practice."

"Who's the policeman?"

"Don't know his name," said Jacob. "He saved me that day of the demonstration, dropped us off at the clinic. My arm was broken in two places. Still doesn't hang right. Who cares? I can still throw a sofa out the window!"

Suddenly two worlds collided. Emil, with three new friends, came walking directly toward them. Niels felt his heart lurch. Emil seemed to be in disguise, so altered was his bearing, his very expression. Two of his companions were tall and swaggering, broad chested. The third walked behind. He was short and muscular, and he walked with a decided limp. All bore themselves with an air of defiance, and Emil had come to match them. He called out loudly, as for an audience, "Hey, Niels! How goes it? What are you up to?"

Emil's look implied a string of questions: *what are you doing with those weird foreigners? How have you sunk so quickly from our brotherhood to those motley two? Aren't you ashamed?* And Niels glanced at Jacob, with that wild red hair and those tiger green eyes, the bony cheeks and jaw—a boy plucked out of the mud and mire. Niels saw Jacob through Emil's eyes, and yet he saw much more.

"Hullo there, Emil!" he called with false jovially. "Good to see you!"

His heart lurched at the swift flicker in Emil's eyes, conveying so many emotions in an instant—disgust, disbelief, confusion. What might Emil say to his new companions? That Niels, his lifelong friend, went slumming with foreigners, Jews? No. Emil would not want to lower himself in their eyes. He would not undermine that Aryan myth they all savored, of racial purity and superiority.

Jacob sat back, casually smoking, gazing off to a middle distance, as if Emil and his friends were mere vapor.

Emil turned away first. His companions followed.

Jacob blew out a stream of gray smoke. "Friends of yours?" he asked in a sardonic tone.

"Emil and I—our families go back very far," Niels replied.

"Is that so?" There was a dangerous gleam in Jacob's eyes, and Niels braced himself against the scathing attack he felt sure was coming.

"Oh, Jacob, for God's sake," Lisbeth said, "stop this grumbling and let's get Niels to our place before he bleeds to death."

"You always exaggerate, Lisbeth," Jacob argued. "Come, then. Let him see our mansion. Who cares?"

The "mansion" turned out to be an abandoned bus that stood in a vacant lot behind the railroad station. "Perfect camouflage," Jacob explained, "with crowds coming and going all hours of the day and night."

They slipped into the bus. Inside, to Neils's astonishment, it was clean, with extra clothing in neat boxes, a few bottled drinks under one of the seats, and quilts neatly tucked under another.

"You live here?"

Lisbeth grinned. "The rent's cheap."

"How do you get away with it?"

"Oh, we know people in high places," she said. "Actually, a policeman arranged it. We have a certificate of occupancy taped to the door. Looks very official—the more seals and ribbons, the better the Germans like it. They never bother us here!"

From a metal box Lisbeth took iodine, cotton, and a gauze

bandage. Niels gritted his teeth as she applied the iodine. "Brave warrior," she said, a low purr, sarcastic.

"What's that?" he asked, indicating a thin vial filled with white powder.

"Nothing you'll need," she said. "Cyanide."

◆ ◆ ◆

A week or so later, Jens came to the house just in time for supper. While they ate, it was small talk, no mention of occupation forces, conflicts with German police, arrests that had to be made to keep up the pretense of cooperation.

Now and then Niels saw his father glancing at Jens in disapproval, his lips pursed, eyes squinting. "How long will be you be staying with us?" he asked.

"Karl!" Mother exclaimed. "Come, we will have dessert."

"Just a few days," Jens replied. He glanced at Niels. His eyes gave warning. *Say nothing.*

Late that night Niels and Jens sat up talking. "I have to 'disappear' for a few days," Jens said. He gave a laugh. "Some Good Samaritans came over to my apartment building and paid a debt to one of my neighbors. Now it is a game of cat and mouse."

"Who is the cat?" Niels picked up his own cat, set her down on his lap, and stroked under her chin, the way she liked. She purred loudly.

"I am the cat," said Jens. "Always. Nobody chases me."

"I have heard," Niels said, "what is done to *stikkers.*"

"Really?" Jens said, brows uplifted. "And, do you know any who qualify?"

Niels shifted uneasily. The cat leaped down, rubbed itself against Jens's legs.

"Not really," Niels said. "One would have to be absolutely certain, wouldn't one? And then—what is done in such cases? Hypothetically, of course."

"Of course." Jens nodded. "Well, the first time we suspect treachery, we send the offender a nice funeral wreath."

"You're joking."

"Not at all."

"And then?"

"The second warning is a bit more explicit," said Jens. "A package arrives, the size of a radio. It is a miniature."

"Of what?"

"A coffin."

Niels stared at his uncle, almost disbelieving. "Is there a third warning?"

"Not really. Third time is a bullet."

Niels took a deep breath, imagining. There was not the slightest trace of a smile on Jens's face. "You are serious."

"I have never been more serious," Jens said. "That business of throwing furniture out the window—that is child's play. Used for unsavory types we don't want hanging around. A real *stikker* is a different sort altogether. There are those who know how to deal with them."

"You?" Niels said, looking his uncle directly in the eye. "You have done it?"

Jens returned the look. "We do not talk about such things," he said.

◆ ◆ ◆

Niels waited for a day when the weather was mild, with a sprinkling of sunshine in the afternoon. The gentle light filtered through the window where Fredericka sat at her sewing machine. She was engrossed, bent over the cloth, her beautiful hair falling over her cheek.

Niels stood in the doorway watching his sister with some sense of objectivity. She was indeed a lovely woman, kind and sensitive and industrious. He could never remember her hurting anyone, even when she was angry.

She became aware of his presence and looked up. "Niels! Hello. I'm not used to . . ."—she gave a slight laugh—"to having you watch me sew."

"We used to play together all the time, when we were young," he said. Memories were flooding back, of their early childhood, outings in the park, coloring pictures, baking cookies.

"Yes," she said absently, examining a seam just completed, cutting off a stray thread.

"Fredericka, there is something I must tell you."

She looked up, startled, quizzical.

"It is about Peter."

Her hand went to her cheek, as if she must shield herself. In her eyes Niels saw the warning: *Don't hurt me. Please.*

"It hurts me to tell you, Fredericka, but . . ."

Slowly, carefully, Niels told her about the *halutz* boys who laid themselves down underneath the train cars, riding concealed for days all the way into enemy territory, hoping to escape. "We think they have all been caught," he said. "Fredericka, I am so sorry. So sorry."

She waved him aside, her eyes turned back to her sewing. She shook her head. "Leave me," she said. "Please. Let me alone."

Niels went out, carefully shutting the door behind him. He stood there listening to the soft *whirr* of the sewing machine, on and on and on. And Niels, who hadn't cried since he was a baby, felt his face wet with tears.

Chapter Seventeen

Fredericka's Diary

I thought the worst thing was not knowing. Niels spoke to me a few days ago, and at first I was completely numb, then devastated. All night I didn't sleep, picturing Peter lying beneath that train, trying to imagine his thoughts, sharing his terror. Was he terrified? No, not Peter. He was resolute. I must remember that. And he was strong. Nobody could kill Peter. Even if they found him, isn't it possible that he is only in prison? This war cannot last forever. Prisoners are released at the end. It happens that way in every conflict.

A week or so before he left, Peter and I went to the park. We stayed there all afternoon, until dusk. And the things he said to me remain in my heart. They always will. "Let us pretend," he said, "that this park is our private place, our house, and that God created all this beauty for the two of us. Look here, Fredericka, at those daisies and the lilies—remember them. Whenever we see a lily, all our lives, let's remember this very moment."

Then he kissed me. It was not a kiss of passion or of desire. It was, rather, long and sweet and pure, so very tender. And when we parted, under his breath he said, "I will always love you, Fredericka."

The way he said my name, the way he always said it, has a different ring to it, a kind of music. I must make myself remember the music, only that.

Today, while I was out walking, I saw a bouquet of lilies through the window of a house. I saw the shadowy shapes of a man and woman moving about, setting the table. Please God, it was a sign. A sign that my Peter is still alive, and that one day he will come for me. Then he will ask the great question that I know has been in his mind. And I will answer yes, without a moment's hesitation. And he will take me to Palestine, and together we will build our lives as pioneers in a new land. I am not afraid. I am not afraid.

CHAPTER EIGHTEEN

Letter from Willi

Liebe Mutti,

I have some good news. I have been assigned a new post, which is quite a fine promotion. According to my commander, I have merited this honor by my loyalty and dedication to duty. Actually, I did not think I had done anything unusual, although I did put in some extra hours, and as Papa always taught me, I try to anticipate the needs of my superiors. Some of the fellows here only think about finding beer halls and cafés where they can amuse themselves.

Now I am working for the new high commandant, Dr. Werner Best, who arrived here last month. Dr. Best was sent to Denmark by Adolf Hitler himself! His task is to keep law and order here, and to see to the dispatching of supplies. I am to be his private courier, at least for now. If I do a good job, perhaps I will eventually become his first assistant. Wouldn't that be something!

Dr. Best is a lawyer, and has had a close relationship with our Führer for many years. It is he who actually proposed that certain people be sent to concentration camps to be reeducated. Dr. Best is a brilliant man, somewhat tense, but that of course is natural for a person in his position. You will understand his status when I tell you that not only is he a member of the Gestapo but is high in the SS.

Several weeks before I was given this new post, Dr. Best tested my judgment by sending me on various errands that required unquestioning obedience and efficiency. Apparently I passed the tests.

I wish you a happy Christmas, Mutti, dear. Of course I am homesick, and I know you worry about me, but I am fine. Do not be sad or lonely, for when you think of me, remember that I am happy in the service to our country, to which Papa also gave his ultimate devotion. Be proud of your fallen husband and of

Your devoted son,
Willi

Part Three

MAY–OCTOBER 1943

Chapter Nineteen

Niels

Their paths did not often cross anymore, but late one afternoon as Niels was leaving school, there was Emil walking swiftly out of the academic office. "Hullo!" Emil called, grinning. "I'm free at last."

"What do you mean?" Niels walked beside him to the bicycle stand.

"I've decided not to take the university placement exams."

"What will you do, then? Are you going into the army?' Niels felt awkward walking beside Emil, with his long stride and the way he threw back his shoulders, like a man on the march.

"I just know that I'm tired of sitting around with books all day," he said. "I want to begin to *live!*"

"And what do you call this?" Niels asked. He unlocked the chain from his bicycle.

"Waiting," Emil replied. "For victory."

"Well, you won't have it from your Führer," Niels said harshly. "He is getting blasted and beaten in Russia. German soldiers are freezing to death, those that aren't ambushed by the Russians and shot."

"Russia is not the whole world," Emil replied. "Look, we have different ideas. That doesn't mean we have to argue about it all the time."

"What else is there to talk about?" Niels said irritably.

"You see! How narrow you are, my friend. You must branch out more, explore life!"

"I have enough exploration, thank you."

"What? Those ragged Jew friends of yours? Listen, that fellow looked psychotic. Did you see the gleam in his eyes?"

"I don't know what you're talking about."

"I am telling you for your own good, you had better stay away from them. They cannot win. To go against the government is treason, you know. *Treason.* Punishable by—"

"Death," Niels supplied. "And who is the traitor here?" he cried. "You parade around with those Nazis!"

"They are not Nazis, they are Danes and proud of it! They just don't want the country overrun by—"

"Oh, shut up, Emil! I'm sick and tired of your tirades!"

In fury, Emil grasped his jacket, pulling him forward. "Just be careful! I tell you, Niels, it can be very bad for you! Those people are gutter rats. They would turn you in for a kroner, for a song. What do they care about you? All they have is their cause, domination, pollution of the race . . ."

Weariness suddenly overcame him. "You have a point," Niels said. "Let's not talk about it. Let's just call a truce."

◆ ◆ ◆

A terrible vibration sent something flying off the wall. Niels heard a crash. He dropped from his bed onto the floor. From far away came a dull roar, *boom, boom,* then crashing sounds, screams. Niels rushed out into the hall, where everyone was stumbling in darkness.

"Don't turn on any lights!" shouted Far. "Stay still. Be calm. Ingrid, come here to me. Fredericka? Kirsten?"

"We're here, Far," they all said. Except for Niels. He was at the window, raising the curtain slightly. Outside, everything was utterly black. Then he saw a glow. Fire.

Planes droned overhead.

"Should we go to the shelter?" Mother spoke calmly. Niels felt her touching his arm. For an instant he recalled that early morning nearly three years ago, when the occupation began, how panicked they were, how confused.

"I think it's too late, Kirsten," said Father. "It's—close. But I think it's over."

Sirens began their piercing, wavering screams, high above the sounds of the staggered explosions. The sirens converged, stopped, began again, great, distressing waves of sound rending the night that had so recently been silent.

"Let's try the radio." Fredericka was the first one in the parlor. The tiny light from the radio was like a beacon. They all crowded around, waiting. A word or two came through the filter of static. Fredericka turned the dial, caught surreal sounds of music, quickly obliterated, a word or two, then nothing more.

"We'll have to wait until tomorrow," said Far. He picked up the cat to carry her to bed. Since the occupation the cat slept only on his feet. A strange, sweet alliance had been formed from terror.

"Where is Jens?" Ingrid wanted to know.

"He has other places to sleep," Niels said, immediately wanting to bite his tongue as his parents gave each other a stern glance. "He is—you know. Sometimes he has to go on duty in the night."

"Quite so," said Mor.

"I think he has a lady friend," Ingrid whispered to Niels as they went back down the hall. "They think I'm an imbecile or an infant."

"It could be a woman," Niels admitted. "Or . . ." He closed his mouth, resolute. There was the one-room apartment in the building Niels and his comrades had visited. Niels was almost certain that Jens was the renter. Probably he was sleeping there. Occasionally Jens came in the night to sleep on the sofa. Usually he was gone before daylight, reappearing like some phantom without warning.

The next day it was announced on the German-approved radio station in clipped, strident tones: "The British air force has perpetrated a ruthless attack against its little neighbor, Denmark . . . with airpower and bombs, despicable act of destruction . . . civilians were killed . . ."

"Friendly fire," Ingrid said, twisting her lip in scorn. "So, the British dropped the bombs, and our people are killed. But they are our *allies.*"

"If we would sabotage the German installations," Niels said quickly, "the British wouldn't have to use their bombs, and innocent people wouldn't get killed when they miss the target."

He realized, with a jolt, that both his parents were staring at him. His mother paused, her teacup in midair. His father turned from the bread-slicing machine to glare at him. "So now you are a student of military affairs," said Far. "Maybe you ought to keep your opinions to yourself."

Later that afternoon Niels went on his rounds. The procedure was familiar now, but there was no getting used to the fear of being discovered. Niels gathered the leaflets and went out, retracing his steps to avoid being followed. He went to the railroad station, enjoying the anonymity, the heightened sense of danger. Here everyone converged—soldiers, Gestapo, police, citizens, and spies. He wished for an action, something bigger than delivering leaflets to public places and shops. He had his "regulars," like Bente Jensen, who tucked the leaflets in between the breakfast rolls, knowing which of her customers were patriotic. It was done in silence, quickly and smoothly.

Niels sat down on a bench in the crowded station. He slipped a handful of leaflets out of his pack, laid them on the bench, and nonchalantly walked away, into the crowd. No telling who would read them and get inspired; the process always left him feeling exuberant.

Outside the station, without plan, he rounded the building to the back, where the abandoned bus stood. From within, a small light glowed, as from a lantern. Suddenly Niels hungered for talk, for information, for the frenetic conversation that only Jacob could offer. He turned, secure that nobody was watching, then rapped on the side of the bus.

There was no answer. He rapped again, on the door. He gave the door a slight push, surprised that it opened, and there in the middle of the bus sat an old man holding a flashlight, reading the newspaper.

"Hello!" Niels called. "Have you seen Jacob?"

"How dare you come here!" grumbled the man, staggering to his feet. He moved like an old bear, stiff from hibernating. "Get out of here! This is my place—shall I help you?" He raised a threatening fist, and Niels dashed out, ran to his bicycle, and pedaled home. How stupid he had been! Of course Jacob and Lisbeth would change their "residence," and do it often. And yet it seemed unfair. Jacob knew exactly where to find him, while Jacob and Lisbeth were as free as birds.

◆ ◆ ◆

Niels studied at night, borrowing Fredericka's notes, thumbing through his books. Meanwhile, his mind was on the turmoil around him. He thought continually of Jens's words, that tossing things out the window was mere child's play. He felt powerless and small. Yes, delivering leaflets was important, but every day, it seemed, the German soldiers on the streets of Copenhagen were growing more aggressive. They conspired together boldly on the sidewalks. German songs blasted out from their green trucks. They challenged people, demanding to see their papers, searching cars, briefcases, and even students' backpacks. Twice Niels was stopped on the way home from school. His heart hammered with dread; he could hardly speak when the soldier barked out the order: "Name! What do you have in that pack?"

"Books. Only schoolbooks."

With his gloved fingers the soldier rifled through the papers and books. For a terrible moment Niels felt that he was going to be sick.

He was dismissed with a look of such pure hatred that it haunted him for days, and anger lay upon him like a burden, a stone.

◆ ◆ ◆

The long, terrible winter gave way at last to a lovely spring, time for final examinations. Niels's mind and heart were torn. *Study, study, for there is a future,* his reason told him. But his emotions lay with the resistance, kindled by the constant flow of illegal newsletters he delivered through the city. He longed to be on his bicycle, bound for the seaside communities of Humlebaek, Hornbaek, Gilleleje, and Helsinor, leaflets in his backpack, a reason for a free day. On the other hand, he was consumed with concern about the oral exams. How could he ruin twelve years of education? Whatever his grade, he would still enroll in university, at least for the first year. But it was also a matter of pride. Fredericka had gotten A's in all her final exams. She was already at university, studying literature and journalism.

Niels was still undecided about his career. For years he had imagined himself following in Far's footsteps, wearing the doctor's coat, attending patients. Now he saw himself rather as a man of action, perhaps a policeman, like Jens. In that case, he would go to the academy. First year at university, he could take a general course, but his indecision tormented him. Everyone else seemed to know exactly what they wanted of the future. His future seemed stuck, like an endless battle with no victories.

After graduation came the celebration, with the entire class dressed in the traditional white, wearing their red-and-white student caps. Niels and Emil and twenty other students from their class shared a large horse-drawn hay wagon, laughing and singing as they rode through the streets. But it was a strained laughter. On the corners stood the Nazi soldiers, staring at the students, weapons at hand. Nazi flags and bunting hung from buildings, reminding them at every turn that they were captives of a foreign nation.

When they got to Kogens Nytorv, where traditionally they would dance around the equestrian statue of King Frederick, a sudden pall fell over the group. Eight German soldiers approached. Two of them stepped out, rifles drawn, gesturing for them to disperse. Niels and his classmates looked at one another, stupefied. They knew that gatherings were forbidden—but this? A dance at graduation time?

Wordless, a soldier grasped one of the boys by the back of the shirt, pushed him down onto the cobblestones, set his boot upon the boy's back.

"Who cares about dancing around an old statue?" Emil called out loudly. "Come, let's go to the restaurant. Only children dance in the streets anyhow."

◆ ◆ ◆

"Thunder!" It was the only curse allowed in Niels's family; he'd clung to it since childhood. The bicycle chain had snapped in his hand. He pulled it off, looked at the ruin, and bit his lip in frustration. Spare parts were almost impossible to find. A trip to the junkyard would take hours, with little chance of success once he got there. Bicycle parts were a rare commodity these days.

His mother, coming in from school, saw his distress. "Doesn't Emil keep a lot of hardware at his place? Why don't you ask him for help?"

Niels only frowned.

"Seems to me you two have not been together much lately."

"Well, with exams and graduation . . . you know how it is."

She nodded. "Give my regards to Emil's mother. I sometimes feel sorry for her, with only one child."

He walked to Emil's house, a fair distance, long enough to ponder memories of their good times together. At the graduation party Emil had been surrounded by girls. Even Fredericka danced with him twice. Emil's charm came from his enthusiasm and his daring. And sometimes, Niels knew, he would say outrageous things, just to impress people. All that talk about joining the Schalburg Corps, the Danish regiment, fighting under the German flag—Niels had challenged him just before graduation.

"So you are free now. You can be a soldier. How about it, Emil?"

"My father is against it," Emil said brusquely. "Anyhow, Commander Schalburg was killed. The corps is not what it used to be."

"Emil, admit it. You never really wanted to fight. What you want is the uniform, to turn girls' heads in your direction. But don't you realize, the Danish girls would hate you."

Emil's eyes narrowed. "Hate? I am not sure. Maybe you mean fear, respect. There is a difference."

It sent a chill through Niels's body. But Emil was a puzzle. When they were children, Emil devised certain torments. He'd pretend to be struck dead, lying prone and motionless until Niels was in tears. Then he bolted up, laughing. "I was joking! Only joking!"

By the time Niels got to Emil's door, he was in a sweat, for the sun was bright, the north wind only a faint puff.

Emil's mother was outside, watering her geranium boxes. The bright red blooms burst against the yellow house like a Gauguin painting. "Good day, Niels!" she called happily. "Isn't it a beautiful day? I thought the winter would never end. Come in, come in. Emil is not here. Off with those new friends of his. You know them?"

"I don't think so. We have different courses, you see."

They went inside to the cool rooms. Emil's mother poured lemonade, handed Niels the glass. He thanked her and drank gratefully. It was almost like being home. Every piece of furniture, every ornament and curtain was friendly and familiar. He gazed about at the pewter mugs, blue pottery dishes, the overstuffed chairs, and paintings of ships and seafaring men with their dogs and spyglasses.

"You are not here so often anymore," she said, wiping her hands on a large white towel. "Well, boys grow up. I remember when you were babies. Time flies. So, you need something, Niels?" She nodded at the bicycle chain in his hands. "You go up to the attic and look around where Emil keeps his junk. I am not allowed to go up there, even." She gave a laugh. "He is a pack rat. I am sure you will find what you need. Poke around. Don't be shy. Take what you need."

After ten minutes of going through assorted boxes and tins of hardware, Niels did find a bicycle chain, old but still intact. Downstairs, he told Emil's mother, "I will borrow it, and as soon as I find another—"

"Na, forget it, Niels. You are family. Listen, it is always a comfort to me when Emil is with you, like last weekend. He told me you had a wonderful trek. A comfort. You are the sensible one, you know. Well, I will tell Emil you were here. Good day!"

"Good day," he replied faintly. He felt hot, almost dizzy. Up on the workbench he had seen the shortwave radio with its headset. He had noticed the position of the dial. Berlin. He felt an ache, like a fist in his gut, at the evidence before him, the deception and the lies. He and Emil had not spent a weekend together in months.

◆ ◆ ◆

He was asleep, dreaming those incomprehensible, violent dreams. There was a tap at the glass. In the darkness Niels groped for the latch and pulled up the window sash. He was face-to-face with Jacob, who wore a dark fisherman's cap pulled down over his ears. His cheeks were blackened with soot. Jacob whispered harshly, "Stork, are you ready for an action? Something real?"

"A minute," Niels whispered. He pulled on his clothes, boots, and cap.

"Hurry!"

"I am!"

Outside, Jacob grasped his hand, pulling him toward a rusted old delivery truck. "Here. Get in. Hurry!"

"Where are we going? What are we doing?" Niels shivered, not from cold, but from excitement. "Who else . . . ?"

"No questions. You will see. If we succeed tonight," Jacob said, breathless, "there is no end to what we can do next. We will have all the power we need."

Chapter Twenty

Julie

"What shall we do for your birthday?" Julie's mother looked up from a stack of magazines that lay beside her on the sofa. She had reluctantly cut her workday to half time. Still, she looked weary. "We have to do something. Sixteen is an important birthday."

"I don't know," Julie said. "Maybe we could all go someplace."

"Yes." Her mother paused. "Where?"

"I don't know."

Her mother sighed. "Well, we will think of something."

It should have been a special time, but the air was thick with tension. Julie kept busy running errands, doing her schoolwork, mending clothes, and teaching Sammy to read, for he wanted desperately to read stories for himself. But beneath the activity was constant anxiety. The sounds of explosions, then sirens, would burst out suddenly, without warning. It was the work of the resistance, blowing up German factories. The Nazis retaliated, demolishing office buildings and rounding up civilians for punishment, a random selection. It could be anyone out on the street; Julie dreaded going out, but she refused to stay home.

One morning she came upon the rubble of a midnight raid.

What had been a three-story office building was now a ruin of twisted iron bars and broken brick and cement. A cavernous hole still smoked. Police and officials circled the site, seeming like ants whose hill has been kicked over.

People gathering at the site, talking. "They were printing illegal papers in there. The Nazis had warned them—you see what happens. It's a miracle nobody was killed."

At school the girls talked about it. "That building the Germans blew up, they say it was owned by Communists," said Ann Marie. "My father says the Communists are worse than the Nazis. Good riddance!"

"Most of them are Jews," said another girl, Bettina, flipping her braid over her shoulder. "The Jews want to run everything, you know, especially the banks."

Julie, standing behind her in line, felt the hot fury rushing to head. *How dare she?* "In case you didn't know it, Bettina, I am a Jew," she said distinctly. "And none of my relatives have anything to do with banking. And we are not Communists, either. We are Danes!"

Bettina's flush spread from her face to her throat. "Maybe you are an exception, Julie," she said. "Everyone knows that the Jews are in this conspiracy." She looked over her shoulder, seeking allies. "They want to take over the money supply of the world."

"You idiot!" Julie cried. Rage filled her utterly. "Do we conspire, then, to get ourselves murdered in concentration camps? What have Jews ever done to you?"

"I am speaking in general," Bettina said, fluttering her hands. "You see, you take offense. But there must be a reason why the Jews are always persecuted."

"Maybe because we don't fight back!" Julie lunged, then struck. With her open hand she smacked Bettina's cheek so hard that the girl reeled. Julie pursued her, like a fighter, but her arms were suddenly pinned back as the teacher and several girls restrained her. "You are right," she screamed. "We do take offense!"

"Stop it! Stop it at once!" the teacher commanded. "Everyone—go to your classes. This is not a show. Go on!" she said, her voice husky. "For shame! Isn't it enough that the world has gone mad? Julie, go and wash your face. Bettina, come with me. Such behavior from young ladies—whoever heard of it?"

Blinded by tears of anger, Julie ran to the washroom to bathe her face with a wet paper towel. She stood at the sink, fighting nausea.

Ingrid's voice startled her. "Julie—are you all right?" She stood there wringing her hands, close to tears.

"Yes."

"Why did you hit her?"

Julie put down the paper towel, stared at her friend. "Didn't you hear what she said?"

"People say things—so what? Let her talk."

"It was hateful!" Julie cried. "Bettina got what she deserved. If that teacher hadn't come to stop me . . ."

"Don't you see that violence never settles anything?" Ingrid said.

Julie blinked. "Why are you against me?" She clenched her fist and felt her silver ring biting into her flesh. "I thought you would defend me. We are supposed to be best friends."

"Does that mean we cannot have a honest disagreement?" Ingrid said. "How can we ever have peace if people don't control their anger?"

"Sometimes anger is correct," Julie snapped back. "If somebody attacks you, don't you think you should be angry? To answer the attack?"

"If somebody tries to attack me," Ingrid said, "I walk away."

"What if they hunt you down? What if they want to kill you?" Julie's voice rose. "Are you telling me you would never even defend yourself?"

"I told you. I would walk away. You weren't attacked, Julie. Bettina was just expressing her opinion."

"Her opinion is dangerous. How do you think the Nazis got so powerful? People said terrible things—others believed them."

"Words never hurt anybody," Ingrid insisted. "Look, I don't want to talk about it. We have to go to class. I simply don't believe in violence. Obviously, you do."

"And if your father were in danger," Julie persisted, "if the Nazis came to shoot him and you had a gun . . . ?"

"I would throw myself in between him and the soldiers," Ingrid said. "I would never use a gun. I don't believe in guns."

Julie looked up at the mirror, where both of them were reflected, she looking wild eyed and disheveled, Ingrid sorrowful, pale.

"You would let anybody attack you and just simply walk away?"

"I hate war!" Ingrid cried.

"Who doesn't?" Julie screamed back. "You think I like war?"

"Let's not talk about it," Ingrid said. "Come on. We have to go back to class."

When they returned to class the teacher was explaining an algebra problem on the board, and Julie tried to immerse herself in the cold, unfeeling logic of numbers.

◆ ◆ ◆

"Come in here a minute, Julie." She went to her father as he sat at his desk in the cluttered little den. A single yellow bulb beamed down from the goosenecked lamp, emphasizing the dark shadows beneath his eyes, signs of stress and sleeplessness. Now he was wrapped in the warmth of his studies. Two canes lay on the desk, one with a brass handle, the other with the head of a duck with bright amber eyes.

"New canes?" she asked, glancing at them.

"No. I'm just responding to an inquiry from a collector in Spain." He took off his glasses and laid them down on his papers. "A letter came from school today. They say you attacked a fellow student."

Julie stood there, looking at the clutter, her father's haven. He was not angry. His tone was one of puzzlement. She was certain he had never hit anyone in his life.

"She was saying horrible things about us. About Jews."

"Yes. Well. And hitting her was, I suppose, a spontaneous outburst on your part." He rubbed his eyes with thumb and forefinger, a mannerism he had acquired since Mother's illness.

"At that time, yes. But now I have had time to think about it," Julie said forcefully, "and I would do it again."

"What does that solve?"

"Nothing! At least it is action. Action! Everyone sits around talking and wringing their hands and wondering what to do, and nobody does anything at all."

"What do you suggest? That we go out and slap everybody who hates us?"

"Maybe that would help!" She paused, hearing her own childish tone. Softly she said, "Why do they hate us?"

Her father chuckled, but without joy. "Ah, that is the conundrum. We have been asking ourselves throughout the millennia. Who can understand hatred? It is a force, an irrational force, like a volcano. Did you know that when I was a boy, I wanted to be a soldier?"

"You?" Julie grinned. It was impossible to imagine her father in uniform, carrying a rifle. She sat down carefully on the small chair with its crewel-embroidered seat. "When was that? What happened?"

"My grandfather was livid. He screamed at me—I remember how near his face was to mine, I could see his teeth, the redness inside his mouth: 'You fool!' He yelled at me, 'You want to fight their battles? Let them kill each other! We don't fight in wars. Don't you how that they conscripted us, pushed us to the front lines—cannon fodder, that's what they called us.' Oh, he was furious. 'They hate us,' he said. 'Never forget that they hate us.' "

"But not the Danes," Julie objected. "Surely not the Danes."

Her father waved her aside. "My grandfather was talking about Russia and Eastern Europe, but he meant more than that. It was a warning. Don't make trouble. Keep to your own business. Because deep down, who knows what they think? Who knows what they really feel?"

They sat quietly in the small room. Julie looked at the books and papers and canes and felt, for a moment, the comfort of being among mere things, objects that had survived all human passion.

"Are these valuable?" she suddenly asked her father

He turned, surprised. "Valuable? Yes, you could say that." He picked up the duck-headed cane. "Each cane has its story; it is part of a life. It has a beginning and an end. It ends here with me, as I tell about it in my papers and share my discoveries with other collectors and museums. About us—what's to become of us, I know very little. So the collection gives me some measure of control, or at least the illusion of being in control."

"Maybe hitting Bettina made me feel in control."

"Did it?"

"Ingrid thinks nobody should ever strike or shoot."

"Look, I am your father. I am not a philosopher. As your father, I must tell you, according to this note from your teacher, do not hit Bettina. Do not have fistfights at school."

Julie nodded, biting her lip. Somehow, she almost wanted to laugh, but it would seem wrong.

"You are like your mother, you know. Always ready for action, taking on the world!"

Mother is not like that anymore, Julie thought. But she said nothing.

◆ ◆ ◆

Aunt Bella sat at the kitchen table in Julie's house, stirring her tea. "Maybe we should make some preparations. Maybe we should we try to get to Sweden. Maybe somehow . . . Sasha, stop fidgeting," she said crossly. "I heard that one man tried to go to Sweden in a rowboat. He drowned."

"Look, the Jewish executive committee has discussed this," said Aleksander. "First of all, there is no reason to panic." The men stood at the kitchen counter, arms folded across their chests.

"None at all," agreed Julie's father.

"What about the extermination campaign in Poland?" snapped Bella.

Father sighed. "Bella, you are always the pessimist. Even if we imagined that the Germans would start an action here, how could we hide seven thousand Jews?"

Aleksander pulled at his beard. "It would not be possible without getting help from the Danes, and who could ask such a thing?"

"It is best to sit tight, sit tight," said Julie's father. "We cannot do anything to provoke the Germans, to give them an excuse for going against us."

Julie's mother spoke out. "This new commandant, this Werner Best, is a conniver. He says one thing to the Danes, another to the Germans, trying to get in good with Hitler."

"But if he does anything against the Jews, he will upset the Danes," countered Father. "He would lose control. People will go on strike. No, his job here is to keep the peace and keep people working so the Germans can get their supplies."

Aunt Bella got up, pacing. "We should try to get to Sweden. I heard Niels Bohr is going to Sweden to petition the king to let us in. Sasha! Get your fingers out of your mouth. Imagine, twelve years old, and he still—"

"We learned about him," Sasha exclaimed. "He won the Nobel Prize."

"Yes, Sasha," said his father with a proud nod. He turned to Aunt Bella. "You see, he knows what is going on." He smoothed down his beard, smiling at his boy.

"Let's hope Bohr will succeed," snapped Bella. She picked nervously at a bit of lint on her sleeve.

"I don't want to go to Sweden!" Sasha shouted.

Julie shuddered. Sweden seemed as far away as India, as impossible to reach, and even if they could get passage, her mother was too weak to travel.

"Be quiet, Sasha!" yelled Bella irritably. She sat down again, pulling her chair with a vengeance. "It is all because of the resistance blowing things up. Those resistance people are criminals! They only make things worse for the rest of us."

Julie looked around at all of them, their faced knotted, their shoulders hunched. Poor Sasha looked miserable.

"Want to play cards?" Julie suggested.

"Sure," said Sasha.

"Yes, go and play, Sasha," said his mother. "You are driving me crazy, eating your nails! Just wait, you will get an infection one day."

They went to the parlor and sat on the rug.

"Let me play!" Sammy demanded.

"Do you know how?" Sasha asked dubiously.

"Of course. I know everything," replied Sammy. "The Giesler boys taught me cards. Everything."

Julie laughed. "Hold on to your wallet," she advised Sasha. "Don't make any bets."

They played several hands of rummy, but Sasha remained preoccupied. Suddenly Bella's shrill voice burst in upon them from the other room. "I tell you, they will not capture me! I have been to the apothecary and bought a packet of—"

"Psht, Bella! The children . . ."

Julie glanced at Sasha. His eyes were wild, and he exclaimed, "I am not going to Sweden. I am not going anywhere!"

"Who says you have to go?" Julie said. "The Swedes don't even want us."

"My mother drives me crazy," Sasha continued. "I will stay here and live with friends."

"Nothing has changed, Sasha," Julie reasoned. "Everyone is nervous now, but the Germans are losing battles everywhere. Soon they will leave Denmark, and everything will be just like before. Soon they will leave us," she repeated, trying to make herself believe it.

"I can't even remember how it was before," Sasha said.

"Tell how it was before," Sammy said gravely. He stacked up the cards and put them aside, and Julie thought how old, how serious he was for a five-year-old.

"Well, there were no soldiers on the street, no green uniforms at all, just our own Danish police, and you know they are nice to everyone who is not a criminal. One time a policeman got Ingrid's cat down from the chimney. Ingrid was petrified that the cat going to slide down and get roasted! It was wintertime."

That brought a grin to Sasha's face, but it was quickly gone. "We used to go sailing," he said. "I remember every summer we'd go to the shore. Now it is all spoiled."

"Yes, Niels used to take us sailing. He's a wonderful sailor, he and his friend Emil. The shops were full of things—new sweaters and shoes and chocolate."

"I like the chocolate best," said Sammy.

"Me, too," said Sasha. He chewed at his thumbnail.

Julie continued, lost in reverie. "There were no shortages. People could go on about their business without being stopped. I remember, one midsummer's night we had a wonderful picnic in the park, people singing and playing guitars and recorders, and we stayed up way past midnight, and, oh, it was so beautiful when the stars came out!"

"Now the stars never come out," said Sammy.

"Of course they do," Julie said. "We are just not going out at night because of the air raids and the soldiers."

"They might as well not be there," said Sasha, "if we're not allowed to see them."

◆ ◆ ◆

Out late one afternoon, Julie hurried into the bakery to buy brown bread and, if possible, butter cookies. "No cookies," said

Bente Jensen, leaning across the counter. "But I have bread and," she whispered, "a small package of butter, if you want it. I got some extra from the dairy. You look as if you could use it," she said with a wry smile. "You are getting skinny."

"Thank you, we'll take it," said Julie. She let go of Sammy's hand and counted out the coins.

She heard the back door slam shut. Bente Jensen excused herself, reappearing swiftly with a package, which she placed low on a shelf behind her. She put the bread and the small bag of butter into sack, then reached behind her and slipped in something else.

Julie went out. There was Niels, about to mount his bicycle, a pack slung across his back.

"Hello, Niels!" she called.

"Julie!" He seemed hesitant, almost embarrassed. "Hi, Sammy. What's new?"

"We got butter," Sammy said.

"Lucky you," Niels said.

"What are you doing?" Julie asked. She had seen the leaflet in the bag among the rolls. She knew that Bente Jensen always provided news along with pastries. But she had never imagined it was Niels who brought the illegal papers.

"Nothing," he said. "Nothing that matters."

"I think it does." She met his gaze. She wondered whether his family knew, supposed they did not. She nodded slightly, with the faintest of smiles.

He gave her a long, searching look. "Ingrid told me about you and that awful girl at school." He gave a crooked grin. "Ingrid says you punched her."

"It was a slap, actually," Julie said. "She was making ugly remarks. Ingrid thinks words are not important."

"Oh, I disagree," Niels said quickly. "I think words are among the most important things in any battle." He paused, began slowly to walk his bike alongside Julie. "My sister sees herself as a pacifist. She thinks that people who are actively resisting are just as bad as the invaders."

"I think they are wonderful! I think they are heroes!" She drew back, embarrassed by her outburst. She murmured, "What does Fredericka say?"

"Fredericka is—well, she is busy. She writes a lot. She reads books. We don't talk about the war anymore."

Julie nodded. "I can understand that. For me, it is different. Because I am a Jew! I am a definite target, more than the rest of you."

"No!" he exclaimed. "We are all the same—human beings. If the Germans persecute anyone, we are all in it together. We fight them together," he said with such vehemence that Julie was amazed. His entire bearing was that of man, not the boy she had known nearly all her life.

"I'm sorry," she said. "I do get excited."

"Nobody can blame you, Julie," Niels said. "I have felt their hatred myself. For you, it must be deeper and worse. And then to hear Ingrid say you must turn the other cheek . . ."

"Well, those weren't exactly her words," Julie said. "But I resent being told I have to keep silent when I want to fight back."

"I feel the same way," Niels said. "My father . . ." He clenched his teeth, then sighed. "Everybody has different opinions. Even people you thought you knew so well suddenly turn out to be—well, different."

"I know."

"So wc have to find new friends," he said.

She looked up, returning his smile.

Their shoulders touched as they walked, and Julie gave Sammy's hand a quick squeeze. They came to the corner, where they parted. She watched Niels until he was out of sight. Then, laughing freely, she raced Sammy all the way home.

Chapter Twenty-One

Niels

Though the evening air was chill, Niels's face was coated with sweat. The muscles of his back and neck felt cramped from tipping his head back to search the sky. It had been the most exhilarating and the most terrifying night of his life. And when it was over, he ached to go back and do it again. There was nothing like it. The anticipation, the roller-coaster plunge of fear at the sudden noise, the rush of adrenaline—it lifted him to strength and daring he had never found in himself before.

It had begun after two in the morning. He and Jacob had stood for an hour in a field drenched with dew, signaling with a powerful flashlight—three flashes and a pause, two flashes, then darkness for twenty seconds, then beginning again.

"Maybe they won't come tonight," Niels ventured, his hands numb from cold, his body aching with tension.

"They'll come," said Jacob. "We were told."

"How?"

"Code. On the radio. Symphony broadcast."

"The code is the songs they play?"

"Not the songs—the names of those making requests. First letter of each name spells out the place. Now you know. Now shut up, Stork. Open your beak just once, and you'll choke on it."

Niels said nothing. He knew that tension and tiredness could make Jacob irascible. Jacob smoked one cigarette after the other, letting the stub scorch his fingers.

"Better be sure the paper is gone," Niels said. "Anyone spotting these . . ." They were American cigarettes, Golden Flakes brand, somehow smuggled to the resistance.

"I'm not an imbecile, thank you," retorted Jacob. But he ground out the butt, tore the paper, and rolled it into a tiny pellet, which he popped into his mouth and swallowed. He grinned at Niels, his face smudged and ragged looking, like an owl's. "There. Satisfied?"

"Yes."

"Want a smoke?"

"No, thanks."

They had waited in silence for a seeming eternity, but when the roar came, at first faint and from the west, Niels's heart pounded and his whole body felt afire, every nerve taunt. Two other men stepped out from the shrubbery, running with Niels and Jacob toward the small lake that was the drop point.

It was all done in minutes—the drop from the low-flying plane, the soft gliding of the parachute, its shell-like silk glistening in the moonlight, then the splash. "Hurry! Hurry!"

They ran and plunged in, wading up to their waists. Niels almost cried out at the shock of the icy water, but there wasn't a moment to spare. "Come on—pull it over—hurry!" Two men on each side of the canister grabbed the handles, pulling it ashore, the white parachute puffing out like a sail behind them.

A tall man wearing a dark pea coat and a fisherman's knitted cap pulled over his ears came out from the shrubbery, nearly blending into the night. He grasped the parachute and with swift, practiced movements bundled it together. He took a knife from his belt, made a gash and ripped off a large piece of silk, shoving it under his jacket. The rest he pushed into a hole already dug, covering it with soil and leaves.

As he bent over, Niels saw his profile for a moment, marveled at the illusion, but then knew it was Jens, for he spoke in his deep, commanding tone. "Come on, boys, heave! Up high onto your shoulders—together now. Don't stumble—watch your feet. There's foxholes and all sorts of junk. One, two, three, four, one, two, three, four . . . all the way to the lorry. Now slowly, heave!"

Perspiration streamed into Niels's eyes. His shoulders ached from the weight of the canister. He was breathless, elated. Jens did not look at him, gave no sign of knowing him at all. And Niels, his heart bursting with pride, kept his gaze forward and spoke not a word.

At last they came to the waiting truck and heaved the metal drum up onto the truck bed. Jens pried it open. Everyone gasped to see the supplies—rifles, fuses, dynamite sticks. "Thank you, Lord!" called one of the men, rolling his eyes in ecstasy.

"Thank the British," Jens said. He gave Niels a sidelong glance. His cheeks were dabbed with bootblack. "Now you two go on home. Good job. See you next time."

"See you," Niels said, as casually as he could. Like Jacob, he thrust his hands into his pockets and sauntered away, as if tonight's job were just routine.

They got into the battered truck. Jacob sat back, lit a cigarette, and exhaling deeply, began to laugh.

The laughter boomed inside the small cabin, catching Niels, too, an outburst of joy and relief and exhilaration. They laughed, bent over, tears flowing down their cheeks in boisterous celebration.

◆ ◆ ◆

The years of patience and restraint were over, it seemed, in a sudden burst of events, one following another so swiftly that there was no time to reflect, only to act. It began harmlessly, with a joke. In the morning a German tank, standing in Townhall Square, was draped with a huge sign: FOR SALE. Danes gathered, nudging one another, laughing. Ridicule was the last straw. Jacob, relating it, hooted, "The Germans did not even think it was funny! The commandant, Werner Best, made a telephone call to Berlin. Reinforcements are coming. The Gestapo."

"How do you know all this?" Niels asked Jacob.

"We have our ways."

"You still don't trust me."

"I trust you, Stork. But what happens if, one day while you are making deliveries, they catch you? And they take you to a place for 'questioning.' What will you tell them?"

"I would tell them nothing!" Niels objected. "Don't you know me by now? Haven't I worked with you in every way you asked?"

"Nobody knows what they would do under torture," Jacob said brusquely. "Look, it is time you knew something. One has to be prepared. If you are ever questioned, you must be prepared to give them something. You remember that apartment building? Where we threw out the *stikker*'s things?"

Niels nodded. "Of course."

"Well, there is another apartment, number seven. It is rented by one of our own people as a foil."

Niels felt his pulse racing. Details were coming together now. Uncle Jens had that apartment, he was sure of it.

"What do you mean by a foil?"

"We have put some things there," Jacob said with a shrug. He lit a cigarette with the stub of another. "Nothing important. An old printing press and duplicating machine, odd leaflets, bogus briefings, a few guns stashed away. Nothing we can't afford to lose. Once in a while we go there and drop off food or trash, to make it seem lived in. Of course, the apartment is rented under an alias, and nobody sleeps there anymore."

"Yes. I see." Jens—what was his alias? He would never know. Jens didn't trust him, didn't trust anybody. It stung, even though Niels knew this was the only sensible way, the way of caution. He had not seen Jens since that night; it was strange and unsettling to have such an ally, one who remained invisible and unreachable nearly all the time.

"So, Stork, if anything happens—if you are questioned, after a while," Jacob paused, drawing on the cigarette, exhaling slowly, "after a time you can give them the address. Then they will let you go."

"How do you know?"

"Well—we hope they will. You are a small fish, after all."

All the rest of the day those words, *small fish,* reverberated in his mind, taunting him. *Small fish—baby face.* He was doomed to insignificance.

◆ ◆ ◆

As he approached the building, there was a sense of danger, like a strange, bitter smell in the air, impossible to identify, but impossible to ignore. At the corner stood a blind man with dog in harness, muttering, begging. Several bills were crumpled in his cup.

"Charity? For me and the doggy?" The man shook his head violently. His hair was a bushy mass, and an odor emanated from his clothing. Across the street two soldiers in green appraised the vagrant, keeping their distance.

As Niels passed, he heard the warning, a whisper, harsh and hissing. *"Don't go there. Don't turn around. Keep walking."*

Home, Niels paced in frustration. In his room he pushed a trunk against the door, went into his closet, and took out the pistol. The cold steel brought a strange, reckless sense of power and comfort. He felt utterly cut off, without a contact. There was no way to find Jacob or Lisbeth or the others who labored in the underground printing office. He did not even know their real names. Frantic, he went out again, walking along the canals, realizing the preposterousness of his thoughts, that he might happen to see his uncle, that he might just run into Jacob at one of the cafés.

At home that night he asked his father, "Where is Uncle Jens?"

His father gave him a sharp look. "I am not his keeper. Why do you ask?"

"Why not?" Niels countered. "He is my uncle."

"Footloose lothario," his father snorted. "Out late every night. I don't see how he can ever get up for work in the morning."

Mother looked up from her papers, correction pencil raised. "Seems to me, Karl, you are jealous of my brother because he can come and go, without being tied down."

"No such thing. I just believe a man has to start accepting responsibility."

"For whom? For what?" Mother asked sharply.

"I do not want to argue, Kirsten," Father said with finality.

It astounded Niels that his father seemed not the least bit concerned about Jens. Well, the two had always behaved like schoolboy rivals, with Mother in the middle.

That night Niels was awakened by a tapping at his window.

He leaped out of bed, pushed the dark cloth aside, and saw Jacob's face pressed nearly flat against the pane.

"Come in," Niels whispered, motioning.

"Can't. Listen, you have to stay low. The Nazis have arrested Lisbeth."

"When? Why? How did they—"

"Shut up and listen! While we were getting the supplies. It was a random search, I think. We can't be sure. Maybe somebody tipped them off. Any one of us could have been followed. We are not experts at this, we are only amateurs."

He means me, Niels thought with terrible dread and guilt. I am the amateur here. He thinks it was me who has been followed . . . God, what will happen to Lisbeth?

"Where is Lisbeth? How do you know this?" he whispered. He wanted to hoist himself over the windowsill, stand with Jacob talking in a normal way. But it came to him in a flash; nothing was normal anymore. In normal times he and Jacob would not even have known each other. He dared not move, for Jacob had that fierce look. At any moment he might take off into the night. And Niels needed him, needed action. He stayed crouched underneath the windowsill, his leg cramped and throbbing.

"We have ways."

"Damn you—tell me!" Niels rasped. "How do you know?"

Jacob hesitated, glanced over his shoulder, brought his mouth close to Niels's ear. "The Danish police get arrest sheets. We have people in the police working with us."

"Jens," Niels whispered. "He is my uncle."

"I know. He has a different name."

"What is it?"

"Target."

"Target?"

"Are you deaf? Listen. They have had her there for two days. She finally gave them the address of the apartment. And she told them it was a policeman who is her contact."

"Did she name him?"

"She gave them a false name. They let her go. They figured they could catch her again anytime they want. She is a small fish and can lead them to bigger fish."

"Where is she now? How do you know all this?"

"Can you drive a truck?" Jacob countered.

"I have never driven a truck, but I can drive, of course. What sort of a truck?"

"Milk."

"Where is it?"

"Just outside. In it there is a white jacket. Go. Put it on. Then we'll drive where I tell you."

"Where will you be?" Niels pulled on his shoes, keeping his eyes on Jacob.

"In back of the truck. My face—I think I am already on their list."

"Why do you think so?"

"Lisbeth had a small photo of me, a thing around her neck."

"A locket?"

"It is idiotic, isn't it, what girls do! Come on. It is four o'clock, time for milk deliveries."

"Where did you get a milk truck?"

"Where else, you idiot? From a dairy."

The inside of the truck smelled strange, wet and steamy. The high seat, the sloping floor, and wide window made it feel like the inside of an open box, fragile and unbalanced. Niels pressed down the clutch, drew his foot back. The truck jumped, like an animal.

"Take it easy!" Jacob called.

The knob of the gearshift vibrated in Niels's hand; the gears ground together, a terrible sound.

"What's the matter with you? You said you could drive!" came from the back.

"This is different," Niels gasped. He let the clutch out slowly. The truck gave a jerk, then slid forward. "There. I think I've got the hang of it."

"It's about time. You dislocated my back."

"Liar!"

Trading insults was one way to keep calm. Still, Niels felt sweat on his palms, and fear rode with him, tight as armor on his chest. The tires of the truck made a neat, slicing sound in the early, dew-filled morning. An occasional slit of light showed habitation. A newspaper boy deftly tossed the folded papers, Gestapo-authorized papers, onto porches. A cat meandered out of an alleyway, looking cautiously right and left before leaping onto a low fence.

"Jacob," Niels whispered harshly, feeling panic. "I don't understand. What are we doing?"

"We are getting Lisbeth," Jacob said tensely, as though his teeth were clenched. "They let her go, but they will try to follow her so she can lead them to others. Don't you understand? Why are you so stupid?"

"But—where is she, then? How can we possibly . . . ?"

"Shut up and drive!" Jacob rumbled. "She is hiding. With a comrade. We are getting her, taking a chance. So do what I say. And for God's sake—*shut up!*"

The drive seemed eternal, with Jacob nagging, reprimanding. "Slow down! Milk trucks don't race down the street. Now you have to stop and bring milk over there. In case they are watching. You have to leave milk!"

"Yes. All right."

"Now stop here," Jacob said at last. "Leave the motor running. Go up to the porch. Wait. She will come out. If you hear anything strange, hit the dirt, fast."

"Do you have a gun?"

"What, you think the RAF sent us bean shooters? Of course I have a gun! Now go on!"

Niels stepped out of the truck, as if he were stepping over the edge of an abyss. His foot hung in the air for a moment. Silence engulfed him. The sudden song of a nightingale startled him, so that he bent double, then straightened. He reached into the truck for a bottle of milk. It felt wet and slippery in his hand. He wondered how the milkman could keep from dropping the bottles, then wondered at the strange irrelevance of his thoughts. In spite of everything, he pondered, the mind does not acknowledge the moment. We race, always, in and out of time.

She was at the door the moment he approached, dressed in black, her face covered with a wide brimmed dark hat. It did not look like Lisbeth, but a strange, angular figure, with awkward, heavy movements, as if her limbs did not belong to her. She said not a word, but pushed past him and into the back of the truck.

"Take off!" Jacob grunted. "Now!"

"Where to?"

"The hospital. Straight ahead three blocks, then right. End of the street. Bispebjerg. I'm sure you know it," he said with an edge of sarcasm. "Don't race. Just go. Go!"

It felt as if he had been driving forever, forever into a dark hole, straining, holding back. He wanted to race. Sweat poured down his sides. From the back of the truck came muffled words. "Are you all right?"

"Oh, yes, wonderful."

"Really—tell me."

"Leave me alone, Jacob. I don't want to talk."

"Tell me, what did they do to you? I will kill them!"

"What do you think? They gave me cocoa and cream puffs?"

"Lisbeth . . ."

At last they came to the black iron fence surrounding the array of brick buildings. It was a huge complex. Neils had not been here since he was a child, coming with his father on some errand. He wondered, had the place grown? Or was he only now aware of the solemnity and grandeur in which his father spent most of his time? He gazed past the iron gates to the wide lawns edged with flowers, bent like small heads in the predawn mist. The broad lawns and occasional benches gave the place an otherworldly look, almost like a cemetery, where war and fear are no longer issues.

"Go past this gate, around to the back," Jacob instructed. They came to an entrance, with an old, dilapidated guard station. It was empty.

"Leave us off here. Thanks. Good-bye."

"Jacob, where are you living? I can never find you. What if I need you?"

"Get out! Go! Park the milk truck exactly nine blocks east of here, by a blue house on the corner. Lace curtains in the window. Leave that jacket in the truck. Do you understand?"

"Yes. And how do I get home?"

"Your problem."

* * *

Niels felt lucky to get a ride with a young intern from the hospital. The fellow had been up all night, too. They rode in near silence, until Niels asked him, "Do you know Dr. Karl Nelson?"

The intern gave him a sharp glance. "Of course. Who doesn't?" His voice took on an edge of suspicion. "Why do you ask? And why are you prowling around so late at night? Who are you?"

"Nobody," said Niels, pulling his jacket up around his neck. "Nobody at all."

Chapter Twenty-two

Fredericka's Diary

I thought about this for a long time, and I kept thinking I might tell somebody, get help and information. Who could I trust? I wanted to confide in Mor, but could not risk it. Certainly, Ingrid would not be the one, little mouse that she is, hiding from reality.

So ultimately I decided what I supposed I knew all along; I had to do this on my own. Once I decided, I realized that Emil is the perfect vehicle for me. He has these horrid friends, and they go to meetings and sound off about Hitler and politics and conquest. Emil is still buzzing around. I see the way he looks at me, how he tries to impress me. Truth is, he is a strong, handsome fellow. Not my type, but I can see that lots of girls would run after him. So, let him think I'm falling for him. I won't be the first girl who has used her charms to get what she wants! Maybe I'm being melodramatic, but this could be serious and dangerous. What would Emil do if he knew I was using him to spy on those low-life Danish Nazis?

I went with him to this meeting, after I let him persuade me for a quite a while. A little resistance is always challenging! Inside, of course, I was terrified. But I discovered, to my amazement, that

I seem to have a real knack for playacting. Or call it deception. It is all a matter of concentration. I made myself concentrate fully on every detail of place and people. I listened so intently that I believe I memorized faces and conversations so well that I will never forget them. That is the secret to spying, I think. Being a blank slate. Listening and remembering. I have no idea how I might use the information I gather, but at least I have begun. And now I am sleeping well again at night. Strange, isn't it, how I am at last finding some peace while I'm in the thick of it. Maybe it's because this is how Peter lived. Maybe for some people there is no peace without action.

The meeting was held in the country, at a rather broken-down old estate, with green fields and fences and barns, and some horses grazing. Ingrid would have been in her element, with those horses!

Well, it was quite a crowd, mostly guys, a few girls. The girls hardly opened their mouths, but were sitting around on the boys' laps, smoking cigarettes, wearing too much lipstick. Anyhow, we sat and talked and drank beer and ate sandwiches and cookies. Emil kept pawing me the whole time—hand on my arm, arm around my shoulders, and so on—as if he owned me, showing off in front of his friends. Those friends! One was a real criminal. He was telling how he stole a car and got away with it! Another one was this very skinny, wiry guy with dark hair slicked back. He wore this odd shirt that hung like a sack, and he had a knife in a leather holder at his waist.

There were a few really ordinary-looking guys. One's family owns a pencil factory. Another one is taking up accounting. They were all talking about getting into the government after the war, assuming, of course, that Hitler would win. They imagined themselves sitting in fine offices and taking charge of things, with assistants to run their errands. What a laugh! Hitler would kill them first. That is what he did to the thugs who helped him get into power.

Some of them started talking about an "action." I acted very stupid and adoring, batting my eyelashes at one of the Norsemen who looked as if he had come off a Hitler poster. "What sort of action?" I asked. "Will you participate? Oh, I'm sure you will take the initiative." He fell for it and sort of straightened himself to look down at me, and he gave that smile—you know the kind they give when they think they are a sex god—and he said, "The Yids. You know what I mean?"

I gave him one of those "oh, you are my hero!" smiles. "Jews?" I said.

He grinned at me. "Oh, yes. They think they are the chosen ones. Well, now we are choosing them for something very special."

So, I believe that Emil and his friends are going to serve as a kind of assistance corps to the Gestapo when things begin "to boil," as Emil says. They are all too young to actually be in the HIPO Corps, but, like the street gangs in Germany, they can create havoc among the people, to help solve the "Jewish question."

I don't know yet how I can use this information. I need to learn something more specific. I don't even know to what extent Emil is involved. I can't imagine that Niels doesn't know the truth about Emil. And yet, if he did, what could he possibly do?

I found out something else. I have not told anyone, not even Mor. Niels has a gun in his closet. I saw it one evening, when I was looking there for some old notebooks I had given him, when he was studying for his final exams. The notebooks were on the closet floor, and behind them was an old fishing box. I got an almost mystical feeling about that box. I knew it contained something forbidden. Maybe I should have walked away, but I am human, after all. My heart was absolutely racing when I opened that box and saw the pistol. It is steel, blue black in color. I started to shiver; I went cold. I think it is a German gun. I don't know how I know. But something came over me, an odd certainty, that he stole it from a German. Now I cannot get it out of my mind. Has he killed someone? Would he? It is so odd to realize that I don't really know my own brother. How well does any one person know another?

Chapter Twenty-three

Julie

In that haze of early morning, with no notion of time or place, Julie bolted up from sleep, her heart pounding as ruthlessly as the beating on the front door. It took more than a moment to find herself, to realize that this was no dream and no repetition of that awful morning over three years ago, when planes battered the morning calm and a sudden rain of green leaflets changed everything.

Julie fumbled for her slippers. From the bedroom Mother called, "Julie! Can you see who that is?"

"I'm going." She remembered now; it was Sunday. Father would stay home from work; she had looked forward to a free day.

Her father appeared in the hallway, disheveled, face puffed from sleep. "Wait. Don't open the door."

"But . . ." She glanced at the hall clock. Nearly nine. But why did it seem like dawn? Yes, they had been up very late with Mother. They had been to the pharmacy for medicine, then the telephone call from the doctor, checking once again. Mother's breathing had been labored. Julie had felt that awful panic, fear crowding out every other thought. *What if she stops breathing?*

Dr. Nelson came. Afterward, they stood in the hall, talking. "Bed rest for your wife, Philip. I don't like the sound of that congestion in her lungs. I will leave this salve. Julie, you rub this into your mother's chest and throat several times a day. It smells strong, but it should be effective."

"Karl, will she get better?" her father had asked.

"What a question, Philip! Do you doubt my abilities? Just don't let her do too much for the next week or so." He winked at Julie. "You know how these modern women are, working, keeping up the household and family—they think they are made of steel. My Kirsten is the same way, never stops."

"She's worried," Julie said, looking directly at Dr. Nelson. "It isn't just the illness. It's the occupation year after year, wondering what will happen to us."

He took Julie's hand, held it for a long moment. "Of course, Julie. I know that. We have to hang on. All of us, wait them out, wait for them to be conquered. And they will be." He glanced at the display cabinet on the wall. "Is that a new one, Philip?" he asked, pointing to a cane with a handsome faceted glass knob.

"Actually, it's one of the first I ever bought. But I like to change the display. This one," he said, "is a weapon cane. The top screws off to conceal a dagger."

"Well, I have heard of such things," said the doctor. "Weapon cane—it would be quite useful."

"Would you like to borrow it, then?"

"Perhaps. I will let you know."

They both laughed, but their eyes were serious.

Later, Julie had dropped into bed exhausted, longing for this day, for respite from weeks of taking care of both Sammy and her mother and trying to remain calm. She and Ingrid had planned to go to Tivoli this afternoon. Maybe Niels would come with them. It sounded wonderful.

"Do *not* open the door!" Father repeated, striding after her in his pajamas, pushing her aside as the pounding continued. "Who is it at this ungodly hour?" he called.

"It is morning," came back the shout. "Past nine o'clock. What is the matter with you, Philip? How can you sleep at such a time?"

"Boris." Her father groaned and slid back the latch. "Good heavens, man, what are you shouting about?" He pulled Boris inside. In the hallway Boris rasped out his message, bobbing and nodding, as if each word by itself were not sufficient to convey full meaning.

"All these strikes and demonstrations! Violence in the streets. The Germans have ordered a curfew. They've issued an ultimatum."

"They always order a curfew," said Father irritably. "Is this why you appear at the crack of dawn? Nobody pays attention to the curfew. Well, come on, we will have some coffee."

"I don't want coffee, Philip! Listen to me. The ships—our ships are all sunk. I have been to the harbor. Sunk! Our entire fleet is gone."

"Boris, what is it?" Mother stood in the doorway, leaning against the doorframe for support. "Is everything all right? Where is Michael?"

"The navy has scuttled the ships. They went down. Over thirty ships. Sunk."

"Why? How can it be?"

"It started early this morning. The Germans attacked the naval base at the Royal Dockyard. Surrounded the harbor. Well, we were not entirely flummoxed, you must know. At the signal, our navy went into action. Sank our own ships!"

"All of them?" asked Julie. She felt engulfed, almost as if she were drowning, like the time she was caught in a riptide, a child of five, terrified until Far came and saved her. She realized that she was gasping now.

Sammy broke away. Julie heard him in the parlor, making chugging sounds, as always when he was playing with his fleet of miniature wooden ships.

Boris went on, his jaw working, as if the omnipresent cigar were clutched between his teeth. "A few got away. To Sweden. Just a few. The Germans blocked the harbor. We couldn't get our ships through—oh, the sight. Sunken ships! Oh, God!" He pulled a cigar out of his jacket pocket, searched for matches.

"Let's have something to eat," Mother said, biting her lip. "Boris, come. A second breakfast. Into the kitchen, come. Julie will prepare . . ."

Julie went ahead and put the kettle on for tea. Nobody wanted the horrible ersatz coffee. It smelled like burned twigs. She set a small loaf of dark bread into the slicing machine and proceeded. The slices were thin, delicate. From the cooler she brought a crock of jam and another of soft white cheese. There was herring from yesterday's supper and three kinds of small pickles. It would have to do. Boris would look around; he might even murmur, "No eggs?" Well, at least there was food to think about, a chance to get her bearings. Now she understood why in any emergency her mother first gathered food. It nourished the body and occupied the mind.

I am turning into my own mother, she thought with a pang. Last night she and Father had sat up late, talking about things.

It had left her feeling hollow inside, aghast at the enormity of what might yet be expected of her.

"Your mother needs special care now, Julie. Thank God it is summer vacation, and you are here. I cannot stay away from the shop. It would look—well, as if we had given up, as if we were afraid. Do you understand?"

Julie had nodded, though she did not understand, did not want to realize that every act was controlled by the enemy.

"It is fine to have Mrs. Giesler, when she is able, but you are family. You are the one . . ."

Mrs. Giesler, out for the past several weeks with her own problems, had stopped in once or twice with a pot of soup and condolences. "I wish I could take Sammy to my house," she said, wringing her hands.

"No, you can do no such thing, with those swollen feet of yours," Mother insisted, "and your husband with his asthma."

It had been Aunt Bella's idea for "the children" to visit her daughter in Odense for a week or so, to get out of Copenhagen and enjoy Rena's large country home with the new kittens and the pond where Sasha and Sammy could go fishing. Bella and Mother had planned it, nodding together: "Yes, they can play as if in normal times. The boys have known nothing but war." But in the end Rena called, frantic about the strikes at the shipyard and the wild street battles with German police pitted against the locals, who armed themselves with bottles and stones and stolen guns.

Another summer destroyed, Julie thought, remembering past summers at the shore, when she had run around barefoot all day, dipping and crashing into the waves, until her mother called, "Come out, Julie, you are turning blue!" They ate fresh fish and potatoes roasted over an open fire. They would bicycle, the three of them, Far usually in the lead, along the lanes and short trails. It was heaven, Julie thought, and we did not know it. The summer after Sammy was born, Far took him in a small basket attached to his bicycle, and Sammy laughed and shouted at every little jog in the road.

Boris and her parents came into the kitchen. Julie poured tea into cups, brought sugar lumps and milk.

"A comfort, that girl," said Boris, giving her a basking smile. "Wish I had a girl. Never had but one child. That Michael."

"Now Julie is looking after all of us," Father said with a grateful look.

"The royal yacht they left alone," said Boris, continuing his tale of disaster. "So, they have some small sense of decency, after all."

"The yacht was probably under heavy guard," Julie said. How could anyone suggest decency among those degenerates? She had been reading about the medical experiments, the stepped-up gassings of Jews in concentration camps, now in full gear. There had been uprisings, attempted escapes, useless against the German might. No, she felt no sense of caution or kindness toward anything German.

Boris gave her a quick glance. He nodded, patting his pockets. "Yes, yes, you are right. They have stolen—everything. It is serious now. They have given the government an ultimatum. They want the death penalty for all saboteurs, effective immediately. Total ban on all strikes and meetings. Fierce retaliatory measures. They have taken hostages in twenty towns."

Father's tone was tentative. "Everyone says we are still in negotiation. We are not at war, after all. Werner Best does not want to upset things."

"Werner Best has been called to Berlin." Boris hung his head down, looked up from underneath his full, dark eyebrows. "He hobnobs with Himmler and von Ribbentrop—even with Hitler. They will demand to know why he has not gotten the Jews out of Denmark and off to concentration camps."

Father thumped his hand down on the table. "Boris, we are still under the protection of the Danish government!"

Boris sat with his had hanging down, his lower lip slack. "It is an illusion," he said softly. "An illusion." He stood up suddenly. "I must go. I will to try to find out—"

At that moment they heard thumping at the door. Julie ran to answer. There stood Michael, perspiring heavily, his face red. "Is my father here?"

"Yes."

"I swear, that old man needs a keeper! Off he goes, never mind the city has gone mad, with arrests by the dozen, people being hauled off—Father! How am I supposed to keep up with you?" he cried as the others came to the door.

"Well, you can't," Boris said, "and you need not worry yourself about me. While the grass was growing under your feet, I was already at the harbor and saw it all! You young people are soft, sleeping away half the day." He gave the rest of them a triumphant look. "I was up. I saw it all. And now I am going to—"

"You are going *home,"* insisted his son, taking his arm.

"You." Boris jabbed a finger Michael. "Keep to business! We must warn people." He turned to Julie's parents. "You should get your children out of the city."

"What are you talking about?" cried her mother. "We are not separating from our children! There's no telling what will happen next."

"It has already happened," Michael said, with a fierce look. "They have declared martial law."

Julie heard a strange low sound from her father. His hand was pressed against his throat. "It is over, then," he said, a whisper.

Michael nodded. "Our government has resigned. They refuse to enforce the German demands. There is no law except German law now. We are totally under their heels."

Nobody spoke for a long moment. Even Sammy's noises had stopped. He appeared in the kitchen, silent, solemn.

Julie asked, "What does martial law mean?"

"Well, they imposed a seven P.M. curfew."

"We can manage that," said Julie's mother dryly.

"Death penalty for saboteurs," Michael went on, with a sharp glance at his father. "The Germans have arrested our army, over four thousand soldiers. Took them all to Horserod Prison. From there"—he threw up his arms—"they will be deported. And all phone lines to Sweden have been cut. We are isolated. The king is under house arrest at Lyngby Castle. And they have arrested Rabbi Friediger and Mr. Henriques, the president of the Jewish community. They are also in Horserod Prison."

Julie looked at her mother. She stood erect, though her figure was frail and thin. "Now," she said, "they will come for us. And there is nothing we can do."

In Julie's mind a scream rose. *Nothing? There is always something!* She looked from one to the other of the adults, saw their agony, their submission. "We have to make a plan," she cried. "Father! Why can't we do something? Go someplace? Get out of the city, as Boris said!"

Sammy rubbed his eyes. His nose was running. He looked up at Julie. "Does this mean we are not going to Tivoli?"

She could not answer.

Chapter Twenty-four

Niels

German soldiers stood guard at every major crossing, at railroad stations, factories, and power stations. Gone from the streets and cafés were the sun worshipers, the young people from offices and academies, sitting together drinking coffee, talking and laughing. Time had run out. Niels, too, felt that sense of urgency, saw it in his own expression when he looked in the mirror.

Jens arrived very early one morning, even before breakfast. Niels had heard his father leaving before dawn, and the girls were still asleep.

Somehow he sensed his uncle's presence in the house. He went into the kitchen, where Jens and Niels's mother sat together at the same side of the table. Their heads were close, their voices low.

"Where have you been, Jens? I've been so worried!" she whispered.

"I've had to move frequently," Jens said. He glanced about, a habitual nervousness. "The apartment—you know what happened. The Gestapo has my name on the list. I've been staying with different friends. Last night I did not sleep. The night before that I was at the dentist's office. Slept for a couple of hours in his chair."

"Yes. You have to keep moving," Mother agreed. She reached out to touch him, perhaps to smooth down his hair as she used to do with Niels. But she quickly withdrew her hand and said, "Well, I've got to be off. I'm proctoring some exams today. Niels, maybe Jens will want to use your bed for a while—he looks as if he has not slept in days. Do you want something to eat?"

"No time, Kirsten." He smiled slightly. "I will eat after the war."

"Ha ha." She turned to Niels. "You eat a proper breakfast," she said sternly. "I don't want you getting sick on me."

"Yes, General," Niels said, giving a smart salute.

When she was gone, Jens took some milk from the cooler, poured it into a glass, and drank it down. "Lisbeth is safe," he said softly.

"How? Where?"

Jens held up his hand, warding off talk. His lips twitched. "Well, I have to tell you, we got her onto the ferry at Helsinor."

"How?"

Jens laughed. "Disguised as a nun. Of course, they always travel in pairs, so we had to get a real nun to go with her. Sister Principia didn't mind—she will stay in Sweden for a while, she said. 'God sends me where He needs me.' She brought only a small handbag. Lisbeth had nothing."

"Only her life," Niels said. "Jacob must be ecstatic. I guess he will want to go and join her. Can you get him there, too? Maybe he will also dress as a—"

"Jacob was caught yesterday, Niels."

"Caught?" Everything in him screamed denial. *Not Jacob—so confident, so clever, so careful.* Questions stuck in his throat; he could not speak.

"They were hunting people down after the Forum was blown up."

"Jacob was involved in that?" Niels exclaimed.

Jens nodded. "Yes. It was—big."

It was just the sort of action that would delight Jacob, setting dynamite charges to blast the German army where they lived. Niels had gone down to the site to join the throng of people marching around the ruin, cheering, until the Germans came with their megaphones and their weapons drawn.

Now Niels felt tears springing to his eyes.

Jens said, "He hurt them, Niels. He struck at the very heart of the occupation. Jacob was wild to do it. He begged to do it, along with some others."

"I would have gone with him!" Niels cried. "I did everything he told me. That night at the parachute drop—"

"We talked about it. He knew you would have wanted to come, but he was afraid. I think he had a premonition."

"Did he say something, then?"

"He said, 'I cannot take the Stork. If anything happened, after all, the Stork has an important mission. So many people would be devastated if he no longer came flying down their chimney. It is quite impossible—he cannot go.' "

"But how did he get caught? What happened? He was always so careful!"

"I don't know. Maybe somebody followed him, gave him away. I don't know."

"How many went?"

"Only a few. Don't press me, Niels. The less you know—"

"Where is he? Can I see him? Can't you *do* something?" A wild sense of alarm swept through Niels, conflicting with the preposterous thought that this was not reality, but some sort of game. In a moment the players would all be called in again, and they would start from the beginning. "Jens! Jens!" he called, overcome with grief. "Jacob is—he is the best. He is like a brother. He is so brave and—"

"They will send him to Theresienstadt," Jens said. "It is what they do to saboteurs—the luckier ones, that is. I went late last night to a friend who knows somebody in the commandant's office. Certain—ah, promises were made. Gifts were given. All I can tell you is that Jacob is alive and on his way to Czechoslovakia in a locked boxcar. But at least he is alive. I have to sleep now, Niels. I can't keep my eyes open. Later, we can talk."

Later that afternoon, the sun came out fully, bathing the streets in warmth, coaxing Niels and Jen outdoors. They walked only two blocks from the house, then in accord they turned back. "It is too depressing to see them swarming everywhere," Jens muttered.

Back in the house, they heard the purr of Fredericka's sewing machine. Jens called, "Fredericka! I have a gift for you."

She came out, expectant, smiling. "Hello, Jens. A gift?"

He reached into his roomy jacket pocket and pulled out a piece of white fabric. "I thought you could make a blouse from this."

"It's beautiful! So delicate, and real silk! Where did you get it?"

He laughed. "Oh, I found it floating on a small lake one night. I'm glad you like it." He lowered his eyes. "If anybody asks you—"

"I know. I know. Say nothing to anyone about anything."

"That's my girl!"

When they were alone, Niels said, "I heard that through the Red Cross packages can be sent to people in Theresienstadt. I think it is the only place they are allowed."

"Yes." Jens nodded soberly. "The Red Cross checks on that

camp; the Germans use it as a model, I've heard. When the officials come, they clean the place out. They need to show some prisoners who don't look like skeletons. I suppose the guards take their share of whatever we send."

"I'll start collecting food in tins."

"And cigarettes. He probably misses those terribly. And he can use them to trade."

"Yes." They sat together in silence, Niels imagining Jacob, how he would miss him. A thought burst into his mind with sickening force. What if Emil was the *stikker?* What if *he,* Niels, had unwittingly led Emil to Jacob? That time they met by accident—perhaps Emil had followed Jacob, spied on him, reported him. At last Niels asked, "If you find out who did this to Jacob, what will you do?"

"Depends on who it is," Jens replied. "These things are subtle. It has to be planned. Don't worry. When we find that *stikker,* someone will deal with him."

"But how can anyone know for certain?" Niels cried. "Being a Nazi sympathizer is one thing, getting people captured or killed is another." His throat felt dry; panic seized him.

"True," Jens said, nodding. "Some are just big talkers."

"But if someone found out that a person was an informer, I mean, what is the procedure? Who takes charge?"

"Niels, you are talking like a child." Angrily Jens snatched up his jacket. "What do you think this is, a social club? You think we have a president and directors? It's everyone for himself, linking up with a few others, doing what they can. Who told you to blow up the postbox? *You* were in charge. You want to be in this, then you have to take responsibility."

"I don't know what to do, Jens! I have nobody to link up with, now Jacob is gone, and you are always hiding!"

Jens jabbed his finger at Niels, and through tight lips he said harshly, "You have a brain. You have a gun. Now figure out when to use each of them."

◆ ◆ ◆

Fredericka reclined against several cushions on the narrow window seat. On an ordinary summer night the streets would be crowded with people, enjoying the open air and the long daylight. "Remember when we'd be out tending our vegetables?" Niels said.

"That was just you and Far," Fredericka said. "You'd be out until nearly midnight, weeding and planting."

"It was the only thing we did together," Niels said. "Now I feel imprisoned."

"Try reading," Fredericka said.

"Thanks for the advice." He paused. "Where's Ingrid?"

"Maybe off with Lars. Or maybe at Julie's house. Poor Julie. They are nervous."

"They have a right to be."

Fredericka sat upright. Her book fell to the floor. She let it lie. "Niels, I have to tell you something."

He waited. She looked so resolute, almost angry.

"I have seen the pistol in your closet," she said. "I was looking for my notebooks, and I—"

"You were snooping," he accused.

"It doesn't matter," she said with a shrug. "The point is, you might as well know that you don't have to go around hiding from me. I know about your escapades, out at midnight, riding all over Copenhagen."

"How do you know?"

"I'm not blind. And some nights, I hear you."

"Does Mor know?"

"I expect so. I have not discussed it with her, or with Far. We each do what we must."

"Except for Ingrid," he said with some bitterness.

"Ingrid is not like us. She will live in the country someday and raise horses and plenty of children; wait and see."

"What about us? Do you see our future, too?"

She shook her head. "What about us? Who cares?"

"I care about you, Fredericka!"

She smiled, then became very serious. "I want you to know, they are planning something, Niels. Something big. I think it is against the Jews. I went to a meeting with Emil. Some of them had weapons, knives and guns. You should have heard them and seen their faces! Like men about to go on a foxhunt, panting for the chase."

"When?"

"I don't know. Soon, I think. I will find out." She paused, looking at him intently, as if she had never known him. "How is it," she asked wonderingly, "that you and Emil are so different? You were always together, sharing everything. Now he is brash and rough and arrogant."

"Maybe he was always like that," Niels said, "but I didn't mind. I never minded that he was the leader and I the follower. He always knew where the fun was, and the adventure. He was always so daring. I suppose I'm a bit of a coward."

"What he is doing now," said Fredericka, "isn't fun. It is not courageous to beat up people."

"Is that what they plan to do?"

She shrugged. "It's what the Nazis do whenever they take over, isn't it? Beat up anyone who doesn't salute them and cheer them on?"

"I think," Niels said slowly, "Emil loves the uniforms and the parades, all that show of strength. He's been reading their literature, about changing the world—in their own image, of course. They want to create a master race."

"That's crazy!"

"I don't understand it."

"Doesn't it make you furious?"

"Sometimes," Niels replied. "And afraid. Emil has always been attracted by extremes. Remember when he was twelve, and he went on that hundred-mile hike? He was lame for a week afterward. When it came to ice fishing or tobogganing, he'd stay out longer than anyone else, never worried about freezing. When we were eight, he decided to be a swordsman and got hold of an old sword and went around hacking at things."

"What did you do?"

"I ran away, of course," Niels said with a laugh. "Like now," he added soberly. "I do my best to stay clear of him. And so should you."

Fredericka pushed back her hair, smiling flirtatiously. "He thinks I will be his girlfriend. I let him kiss me the other night."

"I'm sure the king appreciates your sacrifice," Niels said dryly. "Look, I don't want you hanging around with those types. It's too dangerous."

"You think Emil is dangerous?"

"I don't know. You are playing with fire."

"You don't trust me," she accused. "I can take care of myself, little brother."

"I don't trust Emil," he retorted. "I don't want you hanging around him. I forbid it."

"You forbid?" She confronted him, eyes blazing. "How dare you?"

"I'll tell Far."

"So will I!"

"You sound like a child," he said, gritting his teeth. "Look, you are *not* going with Emil to any—any action."

"Who will stop me?"

He grasped her arms, hard. "If he does anything to hurt you," Niels said, "I will kill him."

◆ ◆ ◆

He found it impossible to concentrate. Nights, he could not rest. He would sleep for an hour or two and awaken with a start to the knowledge that Jacob was imprisoned, maybe starving, being beaten. Someone had betrayed him. Someone. Someone had followed him, knew where he lived, knew he was in the resistance.

The next morning, instead of going to the university, Niels turned on Emil's street. He came to the house and saw that the geraniums were gone. Dark, inert soil lay in the window boxes. He knocked.

"Niels! Good morning. Come in. Emil is gone already, went with his father to the boats. They are fishing, you know. The Germans gave permits to some . . . but you look troubled. What is it?"

There was no tactful, easy way to say it. He stood looking at Emil's mother, her face reflecting years of some lonely search never mentioned, perhaps never noticed by anyone close to her. He bent, suddenly, and kissed her cheek. Then he withdrew, saying, "I am worried about Emil. He and those friends of his . . ."

"Well, I know he is going with some different types."

"I think they are Nazis," said Niels.

"Oh, come, they are boys. You know how boys are when it

comes to guns and such things. They brag and swagger and make all kinds of noise. It does not mean anything, Niels."

"Emil listens to Berlin radio."

"So do we!" she protested, hands raised. "His father and I. We want to hear what that madman is raving about! We celebrate his defeats."

"Not Emil. He is waiting for Nazi victory—hoping for it."

"No, no, you are wrong, Niels. I know my son. He will say things to impress people, to make them listen. I am not saying he is a liar, but he tells tall tales sometimes, makes himself look grand, you know? He wants to be different, so people will listen to him."

She shook her head. "I remember when he was little, how he used to run away and hide, pop out and frighten me to death, he did! He likes to startle people, to get attention. He means no harm. Emil has a good heart. He would not do anything to hurt anybody."

"He hates the Jews."

"How is that possible?" She laughed. Her face creased into countless lines. "He has never cared about such things. You know Emil—his life is the sea, his trekking. He is not deep, Niels, not like you. You are smart. You think about everything. Someday you will be a doctor, like your father. Emil is—he is an innocent, yes, a child of nature. He follows his whims, this way, that way. But he always comes home, Niels. He is a good boy."

Every mother, he supposed, thinks her son is a good boy, even if he is a murderer. He felt no comfort now as Emil's mother patted his cheek, as if he were her own child, and Emil his brother.

•

Chapter Twenty-five

Willi

August 1943
Liebe Mutti,

You cannot imagine what has been going on here. What was once a quiet little country has become a hotbed of deceit and revolt. First, there were strikes all over the country, getting worse every day. Saboteurs have destroyed factories, put railroads out of commission, and stopped shipping from the main port by blowing up a ship in the harbor. It hangs there, its bow straight up out of the water, half sunk, impossible to move out of the way. In Odense, demonstrators beat up a German officer who was trying to prevent a strike.

My commandant, Dr. Best, was hastily dispatched to Berlin to meet with Foreign Minister von Ribbentrop himself, acting for the Führer. The very day Dr. Best left Copenhagen, saboteurs blew up the Forum building, where many of our soldiers have been quartered. Precious lives were lost. Of course we retaliated. You may be sure we put a stop to this revolt with swift and severe measures. Several high-ranking Jews were immediately arrested. It is high time the Danes realize that these parasites must be rooted out from their midst.

We have been too forgiving, too mild. Our commander spoke to all of us and brilliantly explained that the only way to ensure peace and harmony is to use ruthless and ultimate means.

General von Hannecken, who commands all forces here, has declared martial law. The management of the whole country is under the firm hand of my commander, Dr. Best. The Danish government no longer functions. Their navy is sunk. The king is a prisoner in his castle. We are the sole government and the law.

Finally we are being given proper respect.

Dr. Best has elevated me to the position of special courier. I am to be his eyes and ears, he says, when he needs immediate and reliable information. Dr. Best has a plan. Soon the whole world will know it. I cannot relate the particulars now, but when it is put into effect you will hear of it and know that your son played an active role.

As you can imagine, I am proud to be serving under the man who is the highest authority in Denmark. I hope you are pleased by this distinction for

Your ever-dutiful son,
Willi

Chapter Twenty-six

Julie

The fall term began with rain and heavy fog, but Julie and Ingrid rode their bicycles through the mist-filled streets, exhilarated by the thought that this was their last year of *gymnasium*. Next year they would enter University. The world seemed to beckon, despite soldiers and warnings and dire predictions.

One afternoon in mid-September Julie came home to find her mother and Sammy standing at the window in such a way that she instantly knew something was wrong. She burst in the door, calling, "What is it?"

"They came to the library this morning." Her mother was bent, holding her side, as if to stop a pain. "The Gestapo. They demanded the records. We had to give them all our index cards . . ."

Julie stood there trying to understand. "You mean they have everyone's name and address?"

"And they arrested Mr. Fischel."

"Your boss? They arrested him? For what?"

"They don't say for what!" her mother cried. She grasped her hair in her hands. "He protested, but what good does it do? They had guns. I saw. What could I do? Nothing! Nothing!"

"Where were you?"

"In the back room. I could see through the small window. Then I ran to the supply closet and hid there. Did you think your mama was brave? Oh, God, I was terrified!"

"Mother, Mother," Julie went to embrace her, but her mother's body was stiff, withdrawn.

"When they left I—I ran to your father, to the store. It was closed. Where is he?"

Now Julie saw that her mother was trembling, rubbing her hands together as if she had no feeling in them and needed to restore life.

"Did you phone the store? The community office? Uncle Aleksander?"

Mother shook her head. "I—have been standing here."

"Where is Mrs. Giesler?"

"She left already."

"Shall I go and find Uncle Boris? Wait—I will phone the store."

To Julie's relief her father answered immediately. "Where were you, Far?"

"I went out for a bite to eat. What's the matter, Julie?"

"Mother was at the library when the Nazis came. They arrested her boss and took all the records."

There was a long space of silence. Then he said, "I see."

"Are you coming home?"

"Later, Julie."

"Why later?"

"First I must do something. It is important. Julie, stay with your mother and Sammy. Keep them calm."

"I will," Julie said, though she wanted to scream, "Come home! How can you expect me to take charge?"

Julie built a fire, though it was not really cold and she was sacrificing precious wood from their meager supply. But at least they had a place to gather. She turned on the radio and dialed until she found music. Her mother lay on the sofa, wrapped in a blanket, and finally she fell asleep.

"What will happen now?" Sammy asked. "What will Mor do if she can't go to the library? Will she get a new job?"

"I don't know. Maybe she'll stay home and bake and take care of us."

"Mor doesn't like that," said Sammy. "She wants to be active."

Julie laughed and gave him a quick hug.

When Father came home it was already dark. Julie had supper on the table, simple sandwiches and potato soup. He sat down, looking exhausted and pale.

"What happened?" Mother asked, staring at him.

"I took the best pieces and brought them to Henri Frederickson."

"Your competitor?"

"We are friends," said Father. "I told him to keep the jewelry in his vault, just in case."

"And he agreed?"

"Of course. We have known each other for years. I also had another key made and gave it to him, just in case."

Nobody asked any questions. They ate the soup quietly. Then Father said, "We should all go to the synagogue next Sunday."

"Why Sunday?" Julie asked.

"There will be a special service in honor of the king's birthday. Everyone is going; it's to show solidarity."

"Is it safe?" Mother asked, her eyes darting from spot to spot.

Father shrugged. "I feel I should go. You can stay home, Edith, if you like, and the children—"

"I'm going!" Julie declared loudly.

"Maybe we will get some guidance," Mother said. "I guess we'll all go."

In the end her mother was feeling ill; she and Sammy stayed home. Julie and her father walked briskly, their heads covered against the heavy mist that threatened at any moment to break into a real storm.

"Let's stop in for a moment to see Aunt Monica," Julie said. "I wrapped up a piece of pound cake for her."

Father gave her arm a slight squeeze. "You're a good girl."

"What are we going to do, Far?"

"I have been making some calls to see if we can rent a house somewhere up north. Stay out of Copenhagen until this thing blows over."

"What about school?"

"Can't you study on your own for a week or two?"

"Well—I suppose so."

At the synagogue compound, half a dozen men waited at the gate, muttering and complaining to the caretaker who came to open it. They walked quickly around the building to the back entrance, where the cobblestone courtyard separated the synagogue from the Home for the Aged.

Several men held Far in conversation. Julie motioned to him and went across the way to the Home. She opened the door and felt that same heaviness and regret at the sight of the dull walls and the mingled odors of things decaying and the struggle to deny it.

She made her way though the dining room, where she had sat at the piano. The room was empty now. Someone had tossed an old blanket over the piano. It looked like a shroud.

Julie opened the door to the hallway, where several people sat in wheelchairs, nodding idly. An attendant was occupied checking a chart on a clipboard; he started when she spoke. "Hello, I've come to see my aunt Monica."

"Ah, yes, you startled me! You're the girl who played piano. You must come back and do it again. The people spoke of it, oh, so many times, and the next day, even, they were singing."

Julie smiled. "I'm glad. How is Aunt Monica?"

"Ah, coming along, coming along." He led the way down the hall. From the various rooms came sounds—a muted radio, an uneasy snore, a moan. "She is not up much anymore," the attendant said, "and we do turn her every day, to avoid bedsores, you know."

Julie nodded. Inexplicably, her throat tightened; she wanted to flee. But she went through the door the attendant indicated and saw an old, old woman lying on the bed, her face turned toward the door, eyes opening hopefully as she entered. "Who? Who is here?"

"It is Julie, Aunt Monica. I've come to visit. I brought you some cake."

"Cake? Dear child! How can I eat cake? I have no teeth."

"What happened to them?"

"In the glass over there on the table. Never mind. I am not hungry."

"I'll put the cake on the table for later, then," said Julie. She drew close to Aunt Monica, saw how the folds of skin around her neck overlapped, like delicate cloth, crumpled and spotted. "How are you feeling?"

"I have no pain."

"That's good," said Julie. She felt an ache inside her.

"They have given me medicine."

"That's good," she repeated.

A silence stretched too long; time froze. Someone in the next room groaned. There was the sound of metal hitting the floor and a cry, "Nurse!"

"You played the piano. Remember how you played?"

"Yes. Of course."

"Will you play again, child? It was so beautiful."

"I cannot today, Aunt Monica. We are going to the synagogue service for the king's birthday. It is starting already, and I have to go."

"Ah, the king. His birthday? Wish him a happy birthday for me, then."

Julie was about to explain that the king would not be there, that indeed, the king was under house arrest in his palace. But she only said, "I will play piano for you next time I come."

"Ah, yes, next time. There's a sweet girl. And give my best to your dear mother."

It was a regular afternoon service, with prayers and songs, but with special blessings for the king, for his health and safety, and for all Denmark. Nobody mentioned the absence of Rabbi Friediger; everyone knew of the arrest. Rabbi Melchior, the young assistant rabbi, led the prayers: "For all who are forced to labor against their will, for all who are imprisoned, for all who know fear and deprivation, we offer our prayers to the Almighty. May He restore peace to this land and to all His people."

"Amen, amen," rang through the vast edifice with its beautiful Doric columns, the crimson carpet runners accenting the black-and-white marble floor. Julie gazed at the gilded lamps hanging on heavy brass chains and the sconces set into the walls.

The pews of dark wood, the elegant chairs, the carved ark where the Torah scrolls were kept—all seemed to burn their imprint into her mind, this moment mingling with all the other moments of her life when she had sat here in the gallery looking down upon the men. The women beside her seemed familiar, even those she did not know. We are a family, she thought, startled at the notion, for she had heard it time and again, "children of Abraham," but she had never before felt the full impact of that unity. We are a family, we Jews.

She moved to the railing, leaned her arms against it, looking down at the men. Their bodies swayed in unconscious rhythm. Their prayer shawls of fringed satin, their small round caps, glistened in the glow of the lamps, and as they prayed, their voices combined in the ancient chants that seemed to swell, penetrating the very walls. How could their voices not reach to heaven?

Afterward, they walked home quickly and in step, Far grasping Julie's arm. The intense pressure of her father's fingers frightened her. Everyone they passed seemed suspect and sinister. A mist rose up from the wet pavement. A horse tethered to a carriage stood patiently by, its hide steaming. The driver looked away to a distance, grumbling and coughing up phlegm, which he spat onto the street. Julie noticed that Far still wore his *kippa,* though usually he slipped it into his pocket after services. Was it an omission? she wondered. Or actual defiance? She glanced at her father. Surely, without the skullcap, he did not look Jewish, did he? He wore no beard, and his hair was a pale salt-and-pepper blend. His nose was slim, his physique average. What, then, of the certainty of German pronouncements that you could tell a Jew by his looks?

"Far," Julie whispered, "your *kippa.*" She put her hand to her own head.

He seemed startled. Then quickly he slipped the small cap from his head and put it into his pocket. And Julie felt the shame of betrayal.

◆ ◆ ◆

Another week went by, and Far said nothing about leaving the city, and Julie did not ask, for he seemed distant and absorbed. When she felt up to it, Mother busied herself tidying things, opening drawers and removing "clutter," rearranging closet shelves and repapering the kitchen cupboard.

"Why all the activity?" Father asked, always uneasy when major cleaning was under way.

"Don't you know it is almost Rosh Hashanah?" Mother asked, her tone snippy. "For the New Year, it doesn't hurt to be clean, does it?"

"Have you invited people, then?"

"Whom should I invite?" she retorted. "With the curfew, nobody can come out at night. No. It will be only us four, and whoever you might pick up at the synagogue, if they have no other place to go. They can stay on the sofa, I suppose. This damned curfew!"

Sammy flinched. Mother never spoke that way.

Wednesday, just after lunch break, Julie's math teacher came to her. "Julie, would you please come with me into the hall?"

Julie rose, startled.

"Bring your things," the teacher whispered.

Julie gathered her books and her jacket, and an apple left over from her lunch. Something has happened to Mother, she thought. She was needed at home. She would hurry—get there in fifteen minutes. Please, don't let it be too late!

Out in the hall the teacher smiled almost apologetically. "Julie, are you Jewish?"

"Yes, I am."

"Julie, I think you should go home." The teacher stared at her; she wrung her hands. Her eyes were red, as if she were about to cry. "The thing is—we have heard rumors that—that the Nazis are planning something—something terrible. Tomorrow is the Jewish New Year, isn't it?"

"Yes."

"In the evening they will come for the Jews, while they are at prayer. You must hide, Julie! You and your family. Is there someplace you can go?"

"I—yes, I think so," Julie said. She felt caught, crazed, unable to think clearly.

The teacher reached into her pocket. "If you do not have a place," she said, "I will give you my key, and my address, and you and your family can stay until—it is only three rooms, but still—there is room enough . . ."

"Thank you, but I think my parents will—"

"Yes, of course. You'd better go quickly, then. Do you know any other Jewish students? We must warn them. It is difficult, because we do not know . . ."

"I know Helen Lewin and Jonathan Franks," Julie said. She searched her mind. Why didn't she know more Jews? Maybe she did, but nobody paid that much attention to such things.

"Thank you. I will go to the office and find their class schedules. Do you want someone to come with you? Maybe a friend?"

Julie thought of Ingrid. Surely she would come now, if Julie asked.

"No. Thank you."

"Hurry, then, dear. And—God bless you!"

Inexplicably the teacher bent down, gave her a swift kiss on the cheek, and then she hurried away.

Chapter Twenty-seven

Niels

"Niels, see who that is!" called his mother from the kitchen. The doorbell sounded again and yet again, sharp, frantic blasts.

Niels ran to open it and beheld Julie, her hair puffed out and wild, wearing only a thin blouse and skirt, despite the heavy weather. "Julie! Come in. Ingrid isn't here. She went to the grocery—"

"I have to talk to you." Something in her tone allowed no formalities. She stepped inside, gasping for breath. "The Germans are planning an *action.*"

"What?" Niels exclaimed.

"A roundup! Arrests! They are coming for the Jews!"

"Julie, what are you saying?" Niels drew her inside and shut the door against the wind. "How do you know this?"

His mother came in, wiping her hands. She stared at Julie. "What are you saying? A roundup?"

"My teacher told me. She said we have to hide. They are going to round up all the Jews, starting tomorrow night. It's Rosh Hashanah eve. Jewish New Year. They expect us all to be at home or in synagogue, and they will come for us and—" Her voice broke.

Niels felt his head reeling, and he steadied himself, wishing he could put his arms around Julie, hold her safe.

His mother's voice was firm, her stance rigid. "How do we know all this is true, Julie? Is there proof?"

"My uncle Boris. He used to work for the harbor commission. He knows everybody. I called him. He said a man called Duckwitz, who works with Werner Best, found out about the plot. Duckwitz is German, but he is against the Nazis. He told his Danish friends. Now everyone is warning the Jews. We're supposed to hide."

"Hide!" echoed Niels's mother. She shook her head, her expression grim. "My God, that it has come to this! Of course we will help you. We will hide you."

"They have ships in the harbor already," Julie cried. "To take us to concentration camps!"

Niels saw how she trembled. He reached out, took her hand. "Julie, we won't let them . . ."

"Sit down, my dear." Mor led Julie to a chair. "We'll help you. Where are your parents?"

"My mother is home. She isn't well. My father is finding someplace for us to stay."

"Nonsense! You will stay with us. Niels can sleep on the sofa. Your parents will take his room. You and Ingrid—"

"Oh, Mrs. Nelson, thank you. But it is not so simple. We have to find our family and warn them. My aunt and uncle, my grandmother Sophie."

Niels stood beside Julie, watching her struggle, the way she held herself, head high, though her elbows were crushed close to her sides, holding in her emotions.

"Do you want to use our telephone, then?"

"The lines are all dead. Cut or out of order. Even when they are in order, my mother says they might be tapped. I have to go there. I have to warn my grandmother."

"Julie, please do not leave, do not go anywhere now," Mor said, glancing at Niels for support.

Niels felt his entire being surging for action. "Tell me where, and I'll go, Julie. I'll ride my bicycle."

"It will be dark soon. What about the curfew?" Julie looked desperate, blinking, trying to hide the tears in her eyes.

"Your father will be home any minute," said his mother. "You can take the car."

Niels whirled around. *The* car? Never had he been allowed to touch that car, except when Far was teaching him to drive. Now, with its special medical decal, which forgave curfew violation, that car was beyond price. "Will Far allow it?"

"Who is the general here?" his mother countered.

Ingrid burst in, shouting, "Mor! It is terrible, the Germans are going to arrest the Jews. Lars says we have to warn them. He and his father are running to all the neighbors and coworkers. Lars says we have to—"

"Where is Fredericka?" Mor asked, alarmed.

"At Emil's house."

"Is she crazy? She must come back before curfew."

"Mother," Niels said quietly, "if it gets late, I will go and get her. Nothing will happen to Fredericka. I promise you."

Ingrid ran to Julie, dropped down on her knees in front of the chair. "Julie! Oh, my God—what will you do?"

"They will stay here," Mother said. "Until this thing blows over. Ingrid, we will bring the foam mattress into your room."

"I'll sleep on the floor," Ingrid said quickly. "Julie can have the bed."

"It's not going to blow over," Julie said dully. "I know what has happened before. They took Helga."

And Jacob, Niels thought. His whole body ached for action, yet he felt heavy and helpless. "When is Far coming home?" he cried, agitated, pacing.

In that moment his father arrived, bringing a blast of cold air into the house. "What a day!" he exclaimed. He pulled off his coat and hat, flung his umbrella toward the stand. It clattered to the floor. "Have you heard?"

"Yes. Of course. Julie is here," said Mor.

"The harbor has been cordoned off. I drove past there to see whether—we all thought maybe it was just a rumor. A false alarm, to get some concession. But I saw two German ships in the Langlinie Harbor, large transport ships."

Niels gazed at Julie. Her lips barely moved as she whispered, "They will take us away."

"No!" shouted Far. "We are going to hide you."

"You are going to hide all the Jews in Denmark?" Julie cried. "How long can you hide us? Where?"

"Julie, dear!" Far went to her, took both her hands into his. "Do not worry. We will find a way . . ."

"They must be crazy," Mor exclaimed, red-faced, embattled. "How can they imagine that we will let them arrest our friends and shove them into ships?"

"They have been doing just that, and you know it," said Far quietly.

"Never in Denmark!"

"I need to take Julie to her grandmother, Far," Niels said. "Mor says I can take your car."

His father gave him a long look. He sighed, glanced at Mor. She nodded and shaped the words, "Let him."

"Very well," Far said quietly, handing him the keys. He put out his other hand, laid it on Niels's shoulder. "Be careful, Niels. If anyone stops you—wait." He went to his briefcase and brought out a small carton. "Tell them that this is urgently needed at the hospital, to fight an epidemic."

"What is the epidemic?"

A slight smile crossed his father's lips. "German measles."

"I'll go with you," said Ingrid.

"No," said their mother. "We will go to Julie's house and bring her mother and Sammy here. We'll help them gather a few things together."

His parents drew close, speaking softly. Niels saw his father's expression, skeptical and worried. Would Far deny them shelter? Niels could not imagine his parents refusing, but his father's face was stern, resolute.

Niels went to Julie. She sat with her arms clutched across her chest, her expression dazed. "Let's go now," he said softly.

Ingrid took off her jacket and gave it to Julie. "Here, Julie. You'll be cold."

Julie put on the jacket and said, "I'm ready."

"Niels!" His father called him back. He reached into his pocket and took out several kroner.

"What's this for?"

"Just in case you run into any trouble," his father said soberly. "Money talks."

Niels nodded. "We'll be back as soon as we can."

He felt his parents watching him leave, as if they wanted to hold him back. He heard his father say, "I must get to the telephone."

"The lines are down, Karl."

"I will go then to Aage's house and tell him . . ."

The door closed, and Niels pointed to the car, parked just out front. There was a sense of urgency, people dashing into stores, rushing out, stopping one another to blurt out the news. Windows were shaded, doors locked. A few automobiles sped past, horns honking. An ambulance careened along the road, empty.

Did they all know? Had everyone heard the same rumors? Niels saw two men conferring. One reached into his pocket, brought out a stack of banknotes, pressed them quickly into the other's hand.

A mother hurried past with three little children in tow, carrying several bags, obviously bound for the railroad station. Where could they possibly go? A thousand questions surged through Niels's mind. He stopped, realizing that Julie stood at the car door, waiting for him to unlock it. Quickly he bent to do so, held the door for her, then went around to the driver's side, suddenly nervous and excited.

He had never been alone with a girl in a car. In the American movies, boys and girls rode around in automobiles, their hair blowing, and they were laughing and singing. They raced on curved roads, drove along the beaches, or struggled through city traffic, always in pairs.

He wanted to say something, to explain his odd combination of feelings—anger and sadness and excitement, pleasure at being with Julie. For years, she had always been just Ingrid's friend. Now she was different, a separate person, with a certain laugh, a way of looking straight at him, neither shy nor flirtatious like most of the girls he knew. He loved hearing her laugh. He liked her smallness. He liked her hair, the way it curled and frizzed around her face. He wanted to speak, but he couldn't think of anything that didn't sound irrelevant and silly, in view of the task that awaited them. So he kept his eyes straight on the road, as if driving demanded every bit of his attention.

"It's so nice of you to take me," Julie suddenly said. Then she added, "I have never ridden alone in a car with a boy."

Niels chuckled. "Do you know people in America go driving just for fun?"

"I know." She was solemn. He wished he could make her smile, just for a moment.

"I wonder whether their petrol is rationed, too. Where are we going?"

"I will show you. Keep straight—I will show you when to turn. My grandmother lives in a large flat with two other women. Sometimes they don't go out for days. They might not know about this."

"I see." He focused again on the road.

"Grandmother's roommates aren't Jewish, so she might not have heard."

"Well, we'll tell them. We can bring your grandmother back with us." He turned to glance at Julie. She gave him a slight smile. He felt a glowing sensation, success.

"Straight for another two blocks, then left," she said, pointing.

Several more turns, and they came to a broad parkway graced with elm trees, now in fall colors, from pale gold to deep crimson. Across from the parkway was a series of apartment houses, gray stone, with stately windows that indicated spacious rooms. Soon the windows would be shaded with blackout curtains. Now an occasional lamp shone to indicate a carved breakfront, a plush sofa and chairs.

"Here. Stop here, please."

"Shall I come in with you?"

"Yes. Please." She got out quickly and hurried up the stairs, pressed the buzzer, and answered the query in a high-pitched, anxious tone: "It's Julie, Grandmother! Let me in!"

Niels pushed open the heavy door as the buzzer sounded, and from down the hall a woman's voice called, "Julie! Come in. How wonderful to see you. Is everyone well? And who is this?" she exclaimed, catching sight of Niels. "A young man! Why, yes, we know each other. You were taking pictures at the *allsang!*"

Hastily Julie explained her message, words tumbling out rapidly, ending, "So you have to leave, Grandmother. They have lists of everyone, where they live. We did not know how they would use them, but now we are sure they are coming for us tomorrow."

"Tomorrow is Rosh Hashanah eve," Grandmother Sophie said, perplexed.

"That's the whole point!" Julie cried. "They expect us to be home or in synagogue. They will storm the synagogues, then they will come to the houses—"

"Nonsense," said the grandmother, lifting her hands. "What would they want with an old woman like me? I am seventy-nine years old!"

"Sophie, who is it?" called a woman, emerging now in a green lounge coat and velvet slippers. "Ah, Julie!"

"Julie and her friend Niels have come to warn me," said the grandmother with a wry expression. "It seems the Germans want to collect all the Jews and take them away in ships. Well, I am not afraid of them! I have no intention of going into hiding, at my age."

"Sophie, are you sure you ought not to go?"

"Katarina, what would they want with me? Do I look like a

spy or a dangerous person?" She laughed heartily. "Come, my dears. Drink a cup of tea. And I have some macaroons."

The third woman, her hair twisted into small curlers, emerged. She frowned, cocked her head, listening. "What is it? Is something the matter?"

"Oh, Florence, they are starting an action against the Jews, " Sophie explained. "The Gestapo is working in Copenhagen."

"Well, they have been here for years already," said Florence crossly. "We have made it clear they can do nothing to the Jews. We won't allow it!"

"Grandmother, I don't think you understand." Niels saw Julie's alarm, the way she pushed aside her hair, a swift, slight violence. "Father says you must leave. Maybe we can go to Humlebaek, where you rented that house before. You know the people. They would probably welcome you."

Grandmother Sophie shook her head, giving her roommate a curious glance. "Who goes to the shore this time of year?"

"Only for your safety!" Julie cried. "Look, this apartment is in your name. They have the lists! Your name is on the doorplate—they know you are a Jew!"

"Of course my name is on the door. This is my home! Katarina and Florence will help me. If the Nazis come here, we will tell them—"

"They won't care, Grandmother! It's you they want. Don't ask me why!"

Katarina gazed at them, hands clasped before her. "We will protect your grandmother," she said gravely. "We do not allow soldiers to bother her."

Grandmother Sophie nodded, smiling. "As it happens, we are interviewing a new maid tomorrow."

"Florence found her," added Katarina.

Niels spoke up. "You could come and stay with my family for a few days."

"Yes, until this all blows over," said Julie.

"Is your house so large that you can take so many people?" asked the grandmother in mock astonishment, and Niels felt her skepticism, bordering on ridicule.

"If it is crowded, my father can arrange something," he replied. "Maybe you could stay at the hospital."

"But I am not ill! Why would I stay at a hospital when I am not ill? No, Julie, you mean well. And you, young man, are a very dear person. But do not concern yourselves. Julie, tell your parents that I am quite all right here in my own place. Nobody will bother us here. Now, you two better go on home. How did you get here, anyway?"

"Niels's father is a doctor," Julie explained. "We took his car with the decal."

"Ah, a doctor." She turned to Niels. "Is that also your chosen profession?"

He shrugged, annoyed and frustrated. "I have not yet decided," he said coolly. He turned to Julie, imploring her with his eyes. *Do something!*

"Grandmother—please. Do it for me. Just for me."

The woman laughed and put her hand on Julie's back. "Now you are being melodramatic, my dear. Go home. Do not worry about me. I have lived this long because I am quite able to take care of myself!"

"Grandmother! Please!" But the grandmother led Julie to the door, pressing her hand firmly on Julie's back. "Go, child. Go home."

In the car Julie wept softly, wiping her eyes and her cheeks.

Niels wished he could find words to comfort her. He wanted

to stop the car and sit someplace and talk, to console her, put his arms around her. But he dared not even reach for her hand. She might think the worse of him, that he would push himself on her while she was troubled and vulnerable.

"My parents will be so upset," she finally whispered.

"There was nothing more you could do," Niels said, turning to look at her.

She gave a little cry. "Oh, no! You have to stop. It is a security check."

Niels peered forward into the lights. Several German soldiers stood at the side of the road, and one had raised his hand in the universal gesture, *halt.*

"Move over, close to me," Niels whispered. "Quick!"

She moved. He felt her leg against his. Slowly Niels applied his foot to the brake, while his arm slid around Julie's shoulder. He brought the car to a stop, leaned back against the seat, and made himself smile a brotherly smile. *"Guten abend!"*

"Papers!" shouted the soldier.

Niels reached into his pocket, showed his identification.

"Who is the girl?"

Niels made himself grin. "My girlfriend."

"You know it is curfew?"

"Yes, but I had to make a delivery, and I thought—we do not have much chance to see each other," he said. "You know how it is."

The soldier peered through the windshield. Julie moved closer to Niels.

"What is this delivery?" demanded the soldier.

"Something for the hospital." Niels jerked his head toward the backseat, where the small white carton lay.

"I must examine it."

"With pleasure."

"Hands up! Get out of the car. Open the back door slowly."

"I have a doctor's decal," Niels offered.

"Shut up!"

Niels felt his hands trembling as he reached into his pocket and brought out the bills his father had given him. He got out, took the carton, and handed it to the soldier, with the bills held beneath his thumb.

The soldier snatched the parcel, swiftly pushed the money into his pocket.

"What is in here?" the soldier demanded.

"Sputum."

"From what?"

"Diphtheria!" Niels blurted out, the only disease that came to his mind, the only one for which he knew the German word.

The soldier backed away. *"Raus!"*

◆ ◆ ◆

Everyone was already at his house. Julie's family, his sisters, and his parents. They sat in the parlor. A plate of Danish pastries, mostly untouched, stood on the sideboard, together with a platter of cheeses and crackers. Their voices were low, their hands firm in their laps, as if a tone or a gesture might bring about their doom.

"It wouldn't be a bad idea to let me take some tests," his father was saying to Julie's mother. "It's been some time since we've taken an X ray and a blood test."

"What about Philip?" She twisted around in her chair with an anxious look.

"Philip can stay there, too," said Far. "We can put him into a doctor's coat. You can make rounds with me, Philip!"

"But where will he sleep?" asked Julie's mother in a fretful tone.

"We are quite versatile at the hospital," he said with a smile. "It is a house with many mansions."

"You have been hiding people?"

"You might say so," Far said.

"But where? In the surgery?"

"Ah, what a thought!" exclaimed Far with a laugh. "No, we haven't gone that far yet, but we did hide a young woman in the nurses' quarters, then we brought her to Sweden dressed as a nun. Kirsten arranged it with Sister Principia, an old friend of hers."

Niels looked from one to the other. He felt as if he had stumbled into a dream, or into a stage play, one for which he did not know the lines. And yet it seemed that everybody else was cued in, united in an endeavor to which he was a total stranger.

His mother, seeing him, held out her hand. "Sit down, Niels. We are making plans."

He shook his head. Inexplicably, he felt tears stinging his eyes, tears of embarrassment or outrage or relief, he did not know which. "Far," he whispered, "all this time you have been involved, and I thought you were against everything!"

"I'm sorry, son. You know how dangerous this is. I could not tell you. It would have put all of us in jeopardy."

"But Uncle Jens—"

"Your uncle is a good soldier. And so are you. Until this moment, we have not had a leader. It was been every man for himself. But now—now we are a unit. We can work together."

Julie went to her mother and grasped her hand. "Grandmother Sophie refuses to come! She refuses to take this seriously. I tried to tell her . . ."

"What more can we do, Julie?" said her mother. "So strong-willed! Maybe she is right. At her age—"

"What would the Nazis want with an old woman?" Julie's father broke in. "Anyway, tomorrow we will try again to persuade her."

"I will call her tomorrow," said Niels's father. "I promise. Meanwhile, we'd better get you out of here. Tomorrow night, if they do not find Jews in their homes or synagogues, they'll begin searching the homes of resistance people. I'm afraid the Nazis already have their suspicions about me. Doctors are surely on their list. And I must tell you, I have played a few pranks."

Niels's mother chuckled. "Yes, a few."

Julie knelt beside her mother's chair. "So we'll be separated now."

"Just for a few days," said Niels's father.

"Don't worry, Mor," Julie said. "I'll take care of Sammy."

"I know you will, Julie," her mother replied.

"It won't be long," Far said. "We'll get you to Sweden."

"How?" Niels asked. The next moment he regretted having sounded skeptical when he should have been hopeful.

"We are working with others," his father said sharply. "Many people are involved now."

"The new Freedom Council," his mother put in. "People are raising money, finding boats."

"It has been arranged with the Swedish government," Far said.

"How can they take all the Jews in Denmark?" Julie asked, her eyes wide.

"They will take all who can get there," Far replied.

Niels opened his mouth, abruptly closed it again, pushing back the awful objections that sprang to his mind. The harbors were patrolled. The waters were mined. Cannons were dug into bunkers all along the coast, with German sentries on constant patrol. A few people might escape. But there were thousands of Jews in Denmark. *Thousands!*

"How will we do it, Father?"

"Quietly," his father said. "Secretly. By night. We will find small boats and take people across the channel, six, eight, ten at a time. Until we can find passage, we will hide them anyplace we can. In hospitals. Country houses. Clinics. Even in the morgue."

And now Niels understood the enormity of it, and he knew that no matter what the cost, he would help to save Julie and her family, and maybe others. This would be the supreme moment of his life.

CHAPTER TWENTY-EIGHT

Julie

Everyone was gone, Fredericka and Niels at the university, Mor Nelson to her classes, and Ingrid at school. Dr. Nelson had not come home at all after taking Julie's parents to the hospital.

For Julie, it was like sitting on a time bomb. She had awakened in Ingrid's room to the realization that today was the last day. Her parents were hidden at the Bispebjerg Hospital. Tonight would begin that awful time, the roundup of Jews, and there was nothing anyone could do to stop it. Now a terrible sense of urgency overwhelmed her. Last night, as they said good-bye, Julie had made a promise to her mother. They stood together in the hall, alone, and Mother put her hands on Julie's shoulders, looking deep into her eyes. "Keep the family together," she whispered. "Promise me, Julie. Whatever happens . . . Bella and Aleksander and Sasha. I have not been able to reach them. Once the holiday begins, they will not go out. They won't ride the bus. They won't answer the phone."

"I will go to them. I promise, Mor."

"You have to be careful. Take the bus. Mrs. Giesler can watch Sammy."

"Yes, yes, don't worry, Mor, I can take care of everything. By tomorrow night—"

"Tomorrow night." The words hung between them. "It is Rosh Hashanah. Everything was prepared. The table is set. The candles . . ."

"I know, Mother. I will say the prayers. You say them, too. We'll be . . ."

The last word was lost as Dr. Nelson urged them to leave at once.

Now Julie dressed hurriedly, prodding Sammy. "Come on. We're going out."

"It's raining!" he objected.

"So what? Rain is good. People hurry. They don't stop and stare."

Thank you, God, for the rain, Julie thought as she opened the front door and stepped outside. Every bit of her dark hair was concealed under a print scarf, tucked under the hood of Ingrid's blue jacket. She looked hard at Sammy, bundled into his hat and coat. Did he look Jewish? No—he was just Sammy, her little brother, frowning at her now as she took his hand and said sternly, "I'm taking you to Mrs. Giesler's house, and you are to stay inside. Do you understand?"

"Of course. I'm not stupid. But why can't I go to school?"

"You know why," she said harshly. "Don't ask me again."

"Why are you being so mean?"

She took a deep breath, felt the rain on her face. "I'm sorry. Just walk." She kept her eyes forward, trying to imagine that this was an ordinary day, an ordinary errand that sent her hurrying along the streets. After three years of occupation, of soldiers and trucks and roaring motorcycles, of inspections and orders and reprisals, was it any different today? Perhaps the tension was only in her. But it did seem that footsteps were more frantic, faces distorted with the knowledge of impending crisis. She tried to relax her face and hold her head high, as if there were nothing to fear.

Julie had tried to telephone Bella first thing in the morning, to no avail. Perhaps they had been warned and were hidden somewhere. Or maybe they simply would not pick up the receiver, afraid of revealing themselves. Rabbi Melchior had sent out a warning, and it spread throughout the city by word of mouth: *Do not come to the synagogue! Do not stay in your homes. You must find a hiding place. Tell everyone.* Maybe Aleksander had taken Bella and Sasha to his daughter's house in Odense. But maybe Odense was just as dangerous as Copenhagen. Probably Rena was frantically seeking a hiding place, too.

"This is the house!" Sammy said loudly, stopping, pointing. Julie had been lost in her thoughts.

"Yes. I know." She knocked loudly. *Please, let her be home—please, please!*

Mrs. Giesler came to the door, wearing a white apron and a dark sweater, sleeves pushed up to the elbows. "Sammy!" she exclaimed. "Oh, my darling boy!" She pulled him to her, kissed his cheeks, beaming, then weeping. "Ah, I have been so very, very worried! I went to your house last night. Nobody was there! I asked several of the neighbors. Nobody knew where you were. I was frantic. Of course you heard about it. Julie, forgive me. Come in, please!"

Indoors, Julie smelled the fragrance of roasting meat, saw the homey comfort of deep chairs and well-worn carpets, the table where, no doubt, Sammy so often played cards with the Giesler boys. She had never been inside this house before. A sudden wave of regret swept over her as she thought of all the ordinary things she had failed to do. She had often left Sammy in front of the house and told him, "Go on! Go ring the bell. Mrs. Giesler is expecting you." Then she had hurried to some errand of her own.

"Sit down, won't you?" Mrs. Giesler rushed to move some papers, dusting off the chair with her hand, as if the place were not already shining clean.

"I'm afraid I can't stay, Mrs. Giesler. But I was hoping Sammy could stay with you for a little while. I have—some things to do."

"Of course! Certainly. Sammy we will have to catch up on some games, won't we? And I was about to bake a cinnamon loaf. Will you help? There's a sweet boy. Oh, we were frantic," she said, turning to Julie, tucking several strands of gray hair into the large tortoiseshell barrette. "My husband and the boys were running all over town. My Jorgen got the idea to look in the telephone book for Jewish names, to go and warn them in case they had not heard. He was not sure what to look for, but we all put our heads together—Cohen and Levy and Goldsmith. But then, we also know Jews with Danish names—oh, it was so frustrating. But he did find a few and went to their homes. One family was quite alarmed to have him bursting in, begging them to leave! Of course, they probably thought he was a thief, out to rob them the moment they were gone. Poor Jorgen burst into tears, he was so distraught, and he spoke to them so earnestly that finally they believed him, and they went up to a coworker's house. Do you need a place to stay? We have plenty of room," she said, glancing about, her hands fluttering. "There is the sofa, and I can make another bed on the floor; we have plenty of feather quilts."

"Thank you, Mrs. Giesler," said Julie with a gentle smile. "We are taken care of. I will come back for Sammy later today, depending upon—"

"Of course. Sammy," Mrs. Giesler said suddenly, "would you please go out and fetch my watering can? It is a good thing to water houseplants with rainwater."

The instant he was out of earshot, she bent near to Julie, whispering, "What about your mother, Julie? Isn't it too much for her, worrying about—the situation, and Sammy, a young child. Tell your mother, I would keep Sammy with me. Whatever happens, I will take care of him. I love him like my own."

Julie nodded. She did not trust herself to speak, but clasped Mrs. Giesler's hand. How could Mrs. Giesler imagine such a thing, that she would ever leave Sammy?

"I have to go," she said. "I'll come back for Sammy in a few hours."

"Godspeed."

"You, too!"

Alone, Julie hurried along, keeping her steps brisk but not too urgent. She turned the corner, stood for a long moment, pondering. The roundup wasn't until tonight. One thing the Nazis were good at, she thought wryly, was keeping to schedule. Most likely none of them would make a move until the "action" was officially launched. Desire overcame her fears. Home. She had to feel it once more. Purposefully Julie strode to the front door, took the key from her pocket, turned the lock, and went inside.

It was dark. A faint odor of habitation greeted her, and she stood in the hall, savoring, sorting them out—the blue bath crystals Mother liked to use, the smell of baking bread and spices, some pine boughs and pinecones arranged on the round mahogany table in the entry. All the small processes of their lives seemed mingled here.

She stepped softly through the hall and into the kitchen. Several pans were soaking in the sink. On the table was a plate of sliced bread.

Resolutely, still in darkness, Julie turned on the water and scrubbed the pans, rinsed them, dried and put them away. She wrapped the bread tightly in waxed paper and thrust it under her arm. She peered into the cooler, where she saw in readiness the food for the holiday—a large pot of chicken soup, noodle pudding, homemade applesauce. Today she had planned to finish cooking for the holiday meal, with Mor sitting in a chair, giving instructions.

For a moment Julie considered bringing all the food over to Ingrid's house, then she thought better of it. No use arousing suspicion. At least they would have her homemade challah. Holidays, the table was always laden to bursting. They would light the candles, long tapers, and together recite the blessing in Hebrew. Father always sang, explaining, "This was the tune *my* father sang for the blessing over the wine."

Having cleaned the kitchen, Julie went to her bedroom. Her bedspread with the crimson roses, the dolls she had saved from childhood, the books she had read so many times over—all stood like silent memorials to a person long gone. She might have returned from another age, a time traveler, so remote did she feel from her own past.

On her writing table was the photo album. She flipped it open to pictures of the *allsang*. She had planned to collect a few mementos. Now it all seemed irrelevant. She took several pieces of underwear from the drawer, got her own blue jacket, and filled the pockets with panties. Then she left.

In the hall she stood before the display case, pondering. The bird-head cane? The ebony cane with the sterling silver handle? The weapon cane? The one with the carved snake for a shaft? She felt a moment's panic. Which one? Julie reached in and took out the weapon cane with its multifaceted crystal handle. It was a beautiful piece. Nobody would ever expect that it contained a lethal weapon.

Julie stood in the entry, remembering the day three years ago when airplanes sent down their rain of leaflets and dropped German soldiers and munitions into this quiet land. Peter Peretsky had stood in this hallway, talking to her. And just three days ago Cousin Boris came thundering in with his announcement of the siege. The sounds of fear seemed to be collected here in the hallway.

Julie went into the parlor, where her piano stood, its winged top open to the room, like a large sculpture. Gently Julie closed the piano. From the bookshelf she took the holiday prayer book with its maroon cover and gold embossed letters. With the book in her bag and the bread under her arm, Julie closed the door and went out into the restless streets.

◆ ◆ ◆

Julie stood on the bus, making herself feel invisible by avoiding eye contact and pushing away her fear. She was simply moving, riding, seeking her destination like the others. Some were Jews. It was obvious by their furtive looks and mostly by their complexions; nearly all the Danes were blond and blue-eyed. Across the aisle were two soldiers. They, too, made their eyes remote, their expressions bland. And Julie thought, We are all playing the same charade; those soldiers do not want to persecute anyone. They came because their leaders told them they were protecting their fatherland. And now they see families running away with bundles in their arms, the children stuffed into three or four layers of clothes, fearful for tomorrow and its deprivation. So they do not see us, and we do not see them—but for how long can any of us play the game? Doesn't somebody have to win?

The bus turned and twisted along broad avenues, through the heart of the city to the large square where Tivoli beckoned, still bright and filled with the usual crowds. Didn't they know? Were they, too, pretending?

The bus made a wide turn, rolled through a narrow street, came out again past one of the many churches. "Bishop's going to have his letter read at every church," declared one of the passengers, a stout woman carrying a basket of rolls. "Every priest will tell it; to persecute is against Christ's will!"

Nobody spoke. Julie kept her eyes averted. Her stop, at last. She jumped down from the bus and hurried the two blocks to Bella and Aleksander's flat, murmuring to herself, "Be there. Please, be there!"

At the entry Julie gazed at the directory. Three Hansens. Two Petersons. Some Nelsons, written in hasty pencil. Oh, God, she cried inwardly, what apartment is it? She stood there, feeling the utter futility of her efforts. She rang one bell, then another. No response. At last a voice came over the speaker. "Well? What is it?"

"Aleksander Viosk."

"Who wants to know."

"His niece! Please tell me—"

"One minute. I will come down."

Julie waited, swaying from side to side, frantic. She desperately needed to go to the bathroom. Oh, why hadn't she thought of it at home? How impossibly aggravating, that her body kept up its demands when everyone was in danger! She wanted to shout up to the dark windows, "Aleksander! Sasha!"

A man came down, shuffling in slippers shaped like moccasins. Julie saw that one of his feet was encased in a thick bandage, up to the knee. "Sorry," he said, puffing, "I am not so swift, not myself at all. Sorry." The man pointed. "He is up there. Won't answer the buzzer, you see. I can take you. You can call to him—if you are his relative, he will open."

Wordless, Julie followed the man up to the third flight, step by laborious step, until at last they stood before the door number 32. The man nodded.

Julie knocked gently; then, in a wild, desperate rush of agitation, she beat both fists against the door. "Aleksander, Uncle Aleksander, for God's sake, open the door!"

He came, dressed in a long dark jacket, his prayer shawl slung over his shoulders.

"Julie!" He drew her inside, where the odor was musty and forlorn. "How did you get here? Haven't you heard—the danger?"

"Of course! Let me use your bathroom, please."

He showed her the way, looking stupefied.

It seemed an invasion to be here in this private place, staring at such intimate items as toothbrushes, tubes of salve for skin irritations, the frayed white towels and worn nightgown. What if someone were to enter her house, go through her things, finding—what? That she was utterly and inescapably human? Just like everyone else?

Out in the hallway once more, she confronted Aleksander. "I came to get you. We were worried. Where are Aunt Bella and Sasha?"

"She took the boy. They went north on the train. Bella said she would take a room at the hotel in Gilleleje and wait for me there. If she cannot find a place—oh, what will she do? Bella is not accustomed to being without me."

"Why did they go alone?"

"I was in the synagogue with the others. I told her to go. There were things we had to do. I was afraid that she and the boy—I told her I will meet her in Gilleleje."

"You can't stay here," Julie said. "The Nazis . . ."

"Where can I go?" He spread out his hands. "I look like a Jew."

Julie swallowed, hard. Gross understatement, she thought, fighting both laughter and tears. With his bushy dark beard and deep-set eyes, clad now in the satin prayer shawl, Aleksander looked like a stereotype of a Jew from the Middle Ages.

"Well, you must get rid of that beard," said Julie, "and change your clothes to something—hmm—brighter."

"I cannot shave," he said gravely. "I will not. It is against the Torah."

Julie stood facing him, feeling rage building inside her. "Isn't it in the Torah that to save a life one may break a commandment?" Her voice was firm, almost shrill, like Bella's.

"Well, unless when it comes to idolatry or murder," said Aleksander, pondering the fine points. "In that case, a Jew must be willing to die!"

"A beard is not murder!" Julie cried. "A beard has nothing to do with idolatry. *Shave it! Now!*" She began to cry, not from grief, but from sheer rage and frustration.

"Now, now, for God's sake, Julie, don't do that. Don't cry. I will shave. Look, I am going now to shave. Please, do not carry on so!"

When he emerged from the bathroom ten minutes later, Aleksander's face was faintly pink, and he looked altogether different, younger, and in his eyes Julie saw the tears.

"Ready," he said. Under his jacket something bulged.

"What is that?" Julie asked, staring.

"Something necessary," he said. He pointed. "And why do you have that cane?"

"It is a weapon cane. I have saved it for my father. Take it, Aleksander. You can return it to him when we are all together again."

"If God wills," said Aleksander, closing the door behind him.

Chapter Twenty-nine

Fredericka's Diary

Thursday, while we were all gone, Julie did a crazy, risky thing. She went across town on a bus and brought back this relative of hers she calls Uncle Aleksander, but he isn't really an uncle, a nice man, very quiet. He had let his wife and son go to the coast while he stayed in Copenhagen to help move the sacred objects from his synagogue to keep them safe. They took all these scrolls and books and candlesticks to Trinitas Church, and the priest promised to lock them in his storeroom. One thing he kept. It is a kind of horn that they blow on the New Year. Aleksander showed it to us, and he was very emotional about it. Well, we really could not keep him at our house, because Far is on that list of suspected resisters. How could we explain his presence? He does look like a Jew—I hate to say it, but there is this rather haunted expression in his eyes.

Anyhow, everyone knew the "action" was supposed to begin that night. We took Aleksander to Aage's house, and of course Aage was happy to give him sanctuary. In fact, Aage had half a dozen people there already, and his wife was making food for everyone and preparing beds everywhere in the house.

As night fell, we began to hear trucks on the street, and motorcycles. The Germans were shouting, banging on doors. They actu-

ally had trucks parked out front, ready to load on the Jews! Someone yelled out from a balcony window, "What is the matter with you? The people are not here, can't you see? They have gone away for vacation!" Apparently the Germans had been told not to break in the doors of apartments, so they went away. But when we looked out later, we saw them pulling some eight or ten people along the street, and you could see by their walk how terrified they were, stiff and stumbling with fear. We heard later that it was the Rabinowitz family; they were sitting down to their festival meal when the Germans came and hauled them away. Everything was left on the table, even the candles still burning. Their neighbor is Bente Jensen, the bakery woman. She went in later to set things in order—they had not even locked the doors! She says she will keep everything for them until they return. She wept, beat herself on the chest, saying, "I asked them to leave! I begged them to hide! I told them I would trade my apartment for theirs, but they said no, everything was ready for their New Year prayers—oh, they took them away, even the children."

Of course I thought this was the worst that could happen. The next morning Emil came over early. He was excited and wanted me to come with him. I asked him where we were going, what was happening; I did not think we should be out on the street, but he only laughed at me and said, "Oh, but you are a writer. You have to be part of life, a witness, otherwise, how can you write?" I was worried, but I ran to get a jacket and went off with him, because whatever they were planning, maybe I could do something to stop them. How stupid of me!

We went by Dagmar Haus, where the Germans are headquartered, and I thought I would not be able to stop shaking. But somehow I managed, even when all those soldiers came out with their vehicles and their rifles, the Gestapo in their black uniforms alongside the soldiers in green, all looking determined as steel, ready to finish what they had begun the night before.

Then it came out: the first night they had captured very few Jews, almost none, and their commander was furious. They said he screamed and threatened and demoted six officers on the spot. He ordered every available man out on the streets. They had duplicated the lists of the addresses of Jews, and they passed them around, dividing the city into quarters and also reaching to the countryside.

Emil began pulling me along, walking fast, joining up with some other boys, following after the Gestapo. Everybody was in a high mood, as if they were going to a public hanging. I thought they were ridiculous, and I said so—like little tin soldiers, I said, all puffed up but inside, empty. It made Emil furious, and he gave me this murderous look and said, "Tin soldiers? Empty? This is not a game! I have told you to warn your brother, hanging around with foreigners, but you don't listen to me!" We kept following along, until we came to Krystalgaade and the large Jewish synagogue.

Soldiers were everywhere, storming through the courtyard. The doors of the synagogue were already wide open. I looked inside. I think it had been stripped. I have never been there before, of course, but there were no ornaments or candelabra, and the cabinet behind the altar was wide open and empty. Some soldiers were slitting the chairs with knives and smashing the windows. One stood there relieving himself against a wall. I was utterly stunned, unable to speak.

Emil pulled me away and out to the courtyard, and oh, the cries! In my whole life I will not forget those cries. From behind a battered green door, old people came out, staggering, being dragged, kicked, pushed from behind, looking so terrified. Old people! Grandmothers and grandfathers!

One old man grabbed at his little cap. It slid from his head and dropped to the ground. He bent to pick it up. A soldier clubbed him on the back of the neck. The man teetered. The soldier clubbed him again. The man fell. They dragged and pushed him onward, kicking him as he went. Others were hounded out, screaming, women in their nightclothes, still dazed, so frail. One old woman was the worst. She could not walk. They had tied leather straps around her, and they dragged her across the cobblestones, and she was screaming, wailing, "What are you doing? Why are you doing this?" Her head was banging on the stones—oh, it was terrible. She managed somehow to grab onto an iron railing, and she clung there, screaming, "Oh, why are you doing this?" The Nazis cursed and shouted at her to let go! Let go! One soldier tried to pry her hands away, but she clutched the railing so fiercely, he could not get her loose. He took the pistol from his holster and raised it. I thought he would shoot her in the head. But he brought the pistol smashing down on her hand. I screamed. Wildly I sought help—police, Danes, someone sane in this crowd of insanity! But I saw only soldiers and victims, and Emil beside me, bent over and frozen to the spot.

The soldier hit that old woman again and again. The cobblestones were by now red with blood.

Overcome with fury, I pulled at Emil's arm, beat my fists against his chest, screaming every curse I knew. At last he broke away from me, and I lunged after him, still screaming. He had fled to the far corner of the yard. He stood there retching onto a patch of grass, making huge, bellowing sounds. He kept vomiting. I was trembling violently. His face was ash white. He turned and grabbed me. We ran many blocks. I could hardly breathe. We came to the church, burst inside. Emil ran to up to the altar, threw himself down, sobbing, "Christ, oh Christ, forgive me!"

I left him there and ran home, feeling dazed, only half alive. Mor and Ingrid and Niels were there. I screamed it out, everything. Before I got to the part about the church, Niels ran from the house. I think he is going to kill Emil.

I will never write anything again.

Chapter Thirty

Niels

Later, it amazed Niels that he had felt so little anger when he ran upstairs to his room and scrabbled in his closet for the tackle box. The pistol in his pocket felt heavy, but correct, exactly suited to his feeling of certainty. He was no longer afraid or reluctant, but determined and strong, as a soldier who goes into battle knowing he is in the right.

He could hardly remember running to Emil's house, except that suddenly he was there, walking in without knocking.

Emil's mother was in the parlor, seated on the sofa, a mending basket beside her. She was holding a sock wrapped around a darning egg. She looked up, "Niels!"

He said nothing, but ran up the steep ladder steps to the loft, where Emil sat on a mattress, his face to the wall. Niels saw only Emil's shoulder and back and the nape of his neck. Anger came upon him now, crashing like a tidal wave.

"How dare you take my sister into that bloodbath? Did you think she would enjoy watching old people being tortured? What kind of an animal are you?"

The only sign that Emil had heard was a slight shifting of his shoulder.

"You are with them, aren't you. A Nazi. " It was a statement, not a question. "You run with that ruthless pack of wild dogs. Do they pay you as an informer?"

"I don't know what you are talking about," came Emil's voice, low and cold.

Niels raised the pistol, steadied it, and cocked the trigger. "Turn around."

"You have a gun? Then shoot me. Shoot me in the back if you can."

"Turn around!"

"Why? Don't you know how I look?"

"I want to see the face of a traitor! It was you, wasn't it, who betrayed Jacob? He was worth two of you—three of you, ten! He was a man. A hero. Did you know he fought in Poland in the trenches? In the forest? He wasn't just full of talk. He had ideals, something you'd never understand."

"What in hell are you talking about?"

"Turn around, damn you!"

Emil turned. His face looked crushed, like a piece of fruit that is bruised. His eyes were bloodshot. His bones seemed to have melted, for he slipped to one side and his hands hung down, limp.

Niels stood above him, the pistol steady in his hands. "Did you inform on Jacob?"

"Who the hell is Jacob?"

"The man you call worm. Worm and foreigner. Jew. My friend, Jacob."

"I don't know what you are talking about." Emil shook his head. "Maybe I am crazy. Am I crazy, Niels?" He sounded drunk.

"Crazy for girls and uniforms and guns," Niels said.

"You are the one with the gun," Emil said. "Strange, isn't it, how you accuse me of being ruthless. But you are the one with gun, come to kill me. Would you really kill me? And for what—because I am a fool?"

"Did you follow me and Jacob that day? That day we met you on the street . . ."

Emil sighed, looking down at the mattress. "I am so tired, Niels. I feel as if I can never sleep enough to end this tiredness. It is in my bones."

"So you are looking for sympathy. You miserable traitor. Did you follow us? Did you inform on Jacob? I swear, Emil, I will shoot you here where you sit on that confounded mattress . . ."

"Yes. We followed. We saw you go into that bus. But the next time we came there, nobody was living in it anymore. This Jacob, the worm, is smart. He must have known we were onto his place. So, obviously he moved."

"Well, now he has a new address. Theresienstadt Concentration Camp."

"And you think I sent him there." Emil rose slowly from the mattress, shaking himself like a bear rising from hibernation. "Oh, Niels, you never really knew me. I went to some meetings. I heard their talk. We camped out and made big plans. It was exciting! We never really did anything."

"Why did you follow Jacob? Why did you take Fredericka to that roundup?"

"Why did I do anything? I don't know! I don't have motives like you do—I don't plan everything out. I act! I look for excitement and action. That's why you always wanted to be with me, isn't it?"

"Why did you follow Jacob, unless it was to turn him in?"

"I don't know. We were hanging around. It seemed like a natural thing to find out about him. He was so strange. I guess we were going to stalk him, make him nervous. I don't like foreigners. Is that a crime? I don't like weird people. So, kill me!"

Niels lowered his arm. The pistol hung by his side, heavy in his hand. With his index finger, he slid on the safety catch. Emil's eyes flickered at the sound.

"So, you aren't going to shoot me. You, the smart one, solving problems with your brain—you come here to shoot me. I, the fool, I would never harm you, no matter what."

"How many times have you had me in a headlock?" Niels retorted. "How many times did you bloody my nose?"

"Games," Emil replied. "I would never hold a gun on you."

"So, you are the good one," Niels said with heavy sarcasm.

"No." Emil shook his head. "The stupid one. I have never seen anything like what I saw today. How could I know that they meant to beat up old people and drag them across the cobblestones? Oh, the blood—the screaming! I can never forget it. Every night I will wake up and see it again, I know."

Niels stepped back. Emil's agony seemed to radiate toward him, and he wavered between fury and forgiveness.

Emil went on talking and talking, as if he were making confession. Once Emil's mother called up, her voice laden with concern, "Are you boys all right? Do you need anything?" Her questions were lost in the intensity of Emil's explanation.

"I thought—oh, God—I thought it was all about being strong and building a new world. It seemed only natural, that people should be with their own kind. Aryans together with Aryans; we are from the same stock as the Germans, you know. My great-grandfather was German. I thought it was all about ideals, you know, the way any nation holds itself out as being superior—after all, every anthem is that way, praising the beautiful land, the lovely land. I thought all the stuff about concentration camps was propaganda, spread by Jews and Zionists. How could I know they were such brutes?"

"How could you *not* know, Emil?" Niels finally broke through the tirade. "Everyone in Denmark knows what the Nazis do to people, how they invaded their neighbors and conquered countries in a single day."

"Is there a nation in the world that has not made war?" Emil retorted, though his tone was weary, like that of an old man.

Niels stopped. Sweat layered his arms, ran down his side. "We are not talking about war now. We are talking about crimes against civilians. Fredericka told me what they did to those old people, defenseless people . . . and you stood there watching."

"I thought they would just round the people up, move them away. I didn't stop to reason it out! And then we got to the synagogue, and it was so horrible. I did not want to watch. I could not—could not believe what I was seeing. I couldn't believe that I had been in league with those people, drank beer with them, walked with them. I feel filthy." He turned away, head down. "They dragged that old woman—" His voice broke, and he sank down on the mattress, sobbing like a child.

It was nearly dusk when they went down the steps. Emil's mother had called up, timid and tentative, "Don't you boys want to eat something? You have been sitting up there for hours!"

"I can't eat now, Mor. I have seen some terrible things. Don't ask me to tell you."

She only stared at him, nodding slowly. "Well, you are with Niels now. It will be better."

"Yes," said Emil. "Look, Mor, I'm going to be gone for a few days, with Niels. There are things I have to do. To make up for my . . . Well. Things I must do."

"But doesn't Niels have classes in the morning?"

"They have suspended classes temporarily," Niels said. "The students sent around a petition. There is more important work now to do. We all want to help."

"I understand." She nodded, gazing from one to the other. Then she went to the cupboard where the blue pottery was kept. She brought down a tin box, once filled with chocolates. Inside were her savings. She reached in and took out a thick roll of bills.

"I also want to help," she said. She rested her hand on Emil's shoulder. "Good luck, my son."

◆ ◆ ◆

They sat and talked, and it was as if they had met again after a long separation. They avoided discussion of Nazis or war, conquest or occupation. They talked, instead, about living their lives, and somehow those other things lay beneath the surface.

"Well, I think I will travel, you know?" Emil said. "When this war is over. I have always wanted to go to Iceland. I want to see how people live there. If I could get a motorbike or a truck, I would go to the outback and just drive for weeks. You could take photographs."

"We should do it before we get too tied down," said Niels. "If I go to medical school, it will be many years."

"You would be a fine doctor," Emil said. "My friend, the doctor. Somehow, now, I do not think I want to be a seaman. Maybe tours. Do you think after war, people will take tours?"

"I'm sure they will."

"We have to arrange some tours now," Emil said, his forehead furrowed, as if the entire responsibility rested upon him. "We must get those people to Sweden. Grandfather can help us."

"And Jens."

For Niels, a single thought dominated every moment: rescue.

Whatever had happened until now, whatever might happen afterward, this was the time for action. After midnight, with only candles for illumination, they sat in Niels's kitchen, deliberating. Jens outlined the plan for the rest of them, Far and his friend Aage, Fredericka, Emil, and Niels. Ingrid stood in the doorway, leaning against the doorframe. His mother served endless cups of tea and biscuits. All day they had been moving through the city finding Jews, whisking them into homes, apartments, local hospitals, warehouses, and shops.

"We have to move north, to the coast," Jens said. Thick stubble on his cheeks gave him a rough, burly look, making his deep blue eyes even more prominent, almost glowing. "We can take them various ways—we have a few trucks, a few cars, like Karl's, with the doctor's decal . . ."

"And then, of course," Far put in, "ambulances."

"And a hearse," added Mor. "We can get taxis to drive slowly behind the hearse, a funeral cortege."

"Funeral is a good idea," Niels said. "I could take Julie and Sammy. We can get black armbands, as if we were going to a funeral of a relative . . ."

"I'm going with you," Emil said. "If we are stopped, I can prove I have family in Helsinor. We could say it is my grandmother's funeral. And you are all friends of the family."

"Fine," Niels said, nodding. "So there will be five of us."

"I'm coming, too," Fredericka said. She bit her lip nervously, refusing to look at Emil, but Niels saw the defiant lift of her chin.

"I suppose it would seem more natural, having the girls along," said Far. "Fredericka with her blond hair . . ."

"And me," said Ingrid.

Everyone turned to look at her in surprise. "I thought you didn't want to get involved in such matters," Fredericka said tartly.

"That was before," Ingrid retorted.

Emil broke in. "We can stay at my grandfather's house in case we need to spend the night." He kept his distance from Fredericka, now and then stealing a glance at her.

"How do you know your grandfather will agree?" Niels asked.

"I called him on the telephone."

"What!" Jens cried. "How could you do such a thing? The phones could be tapped. Good heavens, did you call from here?"

Emil stood up, and Niels saw the old assertiveness in his posture and in the waving of his hands. "Of course, I am not so stupid! I called from my house. I said, 'I am bringing a large basket of bread for the people. We will make delivery tomorrow.'"

"And he understood you?" Jens said with a grin.

"Grandfather may be old, but he is not dense. He said, 'I will prepare everything for the party, then.'"

"Good. You will leave early in the morning. The funeral would be at noon. Karl, you pick up the parents at the hospital. How is Mrs. Weinstein?"

"In fair condition, I suppose. I have given her—something."

◆ ◆ ◆

Niels had traveled this road before, too many times to count. Summers, everyone went to the shore, at least for a day or two, sometimes for weeks at a time, basking in the sun, burrowing in the sand, pretending winter was banished for good.

The road north wound around coves and slim-treed forests of aspen and elm. It took them past summer homes with wide front porches, green lawns, stone walls, and parapets. Usually, this journey launched Niels into a special mood of anticipation and pleasure. Now there was only apprehension. For all the excitement and nervy posturing that had played a prelude in this action, the reality held him gripped in fear.

Driving, Niels kept his eyes straight forward, squinting against the spattering sunlight. Fredericka sat beside him, gazing intently to the front, silent and tense. In the back were Emil, Ingrid, and Julie, with Sammy locked in a sleep so deep that he snored lightly, making purring sounds.

In the end, it was decided that Ingrid and Fredericka would return to Copenhagen by train to help bring others to the coast. This trip would help them to learn what to expect, where there might be trouble, the route to take.

"Wear dark clothes," Niels had instructed everyone. "We're going to a funeral after all. No smiling or happy faces."

"What about Sammy?" Fredericka asked.

"He will be asleep."

"How do you know?" Julie asked.

"I guarantee it." Niels showed her the bottle of small white pills his father had given him. "Julie, you will put one of these into his porridge."

She had nodded. "All right." Now she asked, "What about my uncle Aleksander?"

"Aage is taking him on his motorcycle. With a leather jacket and a dark hat with ear muffs, he will get through just fine. Don't worry. We will meet them at the hotel in Gilleleje."

"Whose funeral do we say it is?" asked Ingrid, frowning in concentration.

"My grandmother's," said Emil.

"I thought she died years ago."

"She died again. So what?"

Niels moved his shoulders and stretched his neck, trying to displace the strain in his muscles. He was keenly aware of Emil sitting behind him with a gun.

Before they left, he had taken Emil aside. "Keep this ready," he said, handing him the pistol. "You will sit in the backseat, behind me. If anyone should stop us, I will have to get out of the car. If they saw me with a gun, it would all be over. But you—just wait in the back. If there is trouble, then you come out."

"What trouble?" Emil's face became red, as if he were sweating.

"If they try to prevent us," Niels said, with a steady gaze, "you use the pistol. Aim for the center of the chest."

"You want me to shoot?"

"Yes, if you have to. Are you up to it?"

Emil held the pistol in his hand, as if to assess its potential. He pulled back the clip, peered into the chamber. "It's loaded," he said in wonderment.

"Of course."

Niels saw the drops of sweat on Emil's upper lip, the resolute expression on his face as he tucked the pistol into his belt, covering it with his jacket. He was different now, hesitant in his movements, no longer giving orders. And Niels could imagine the demons that circled in Emil's mind.

"Stop!" Fredericka suddenly said, straining forward in her seat. "There's a patrol ahead. Trucks. You'd better turn around."

"Then what?"

"There's another road, a bit inland," Emil said. "A dirt road. It will be better. Less traveled. Don't you remember? We used to go on our bicycles."

Niels spun the car around, made the first right turn through a long track of fields and farmhouses. A group of Holstein cattle stood under a tree, some chewing, turning to stare at the car. He heard a slight sigh from Fredericka, knew her thoughts were of Peter and his farm. He glanced around; Ingrid was looking back at the pastoral scene. Only Emil sat rigid, lost in his thoughts.

"Going this way," Niels said, "won't we miss Helsinor?"

"We'll come out at Gilleleje, then go south to Grandfather's. Just a few kilometers out of the way."

"Bella should be at the hotel in Gilleleje," said Julie. "The one just on the coast, not far from the church."

"I know the place," said Niels. "We can stop and see."

"Thank you," Julie said gratefully. She shifted her weight. "My leg has gone to sleep. Sammy's heavy."

"Here, let me," said Ingrid.

Niels heard the sounds of people rearranging themselves, except for Emil, who kept his stiff pose behind him, probably his hand on the gun. They rolled into the town of Gilleleje, past the railroad station and the main square, where several soldiers lounged, and a kiosk stood, plastered with Nazi posters.

The instant they crossed the square, two soldiers blocked their way. "Halt!"

One was heavyset, with a Hitler mustache and thick dark eyebrows. *"Austeigen!"* he commanded, with his hand on the side of the car.

Everyone stiffened. Niels could feel their fear. He made himself relax, leaning out the window. "Hello, is something the matter?"

"Raus!" The soldier gestured with his rifle, peering into the car. "Where are you going?"

"We are going to a funeral. Our grandmother."

"Here in Gilleleje?"

"Yes. The service will be at the church over there." Niels held his breath as he looked over to the church with its whitewashed exterior and red roof, small but massive, a Norman edifice fortified against winter with thick walls and small windows. And he was astounded to see a line of automobiles making their way toward the church. Some people already stood assembled there, dressed in somber clothes, wearing black armbands.

"That is our group," Niels said. He made his voice firm, authoritative. "The funeral is starting." His mind flitted to Jacob. Everything could change in a moment.

The mustached soldier seemed satisfied. But his partner called out, "Open the trunk!"

Niels turned, glancing at Emil as he moved to the back of the car. "Only some blankets and clothing," he said.

"For whom are they?" bellowed the soldier.

"For us," said Niels. "We are sleeping at my grandfather's house tonight. He has not enough blankets for so many people. It is our custom for everyone to spend the night after a funeral." He met the soldier's gaze without blinking.

The soldier grunted and motioned for Niels to shut the trunk. The one with the mustache peered into the car once more. Niels felt his heart pounding against his chest. The Nazi motioned for Niels to proceed while he strode out to the front of the square and began directing traffic with swift, military gestures.

Niels looked back at Julie. Their eyes met. Though neither of them spoke, it felt as if they were in deep conversation, just beginning to know each other, really.

Chapter Thirty-one

Julie

It felt horrible to have to hide, sitting in the car with her head low, face turned away from the windows—a fugitive in her own land. Julie felt marked, as if the word *Jew* were tattooed on her forehead. She knew how those people in other lands must have felt when the yellow star or patch was forced upon them. It branded them, singled them out, like animals marked for the slaughterhouse.

They drove slowly to the church, mindful that the German guards would keep an eye on their car. In front of the church stood several soldiers, silent and still. They looked so young, Julie thought, and uncomfortable. Maybe they wished they were home, and not among these milling crowds, people looking so desperate, as if they had indeed lost a beloved relative and could hardly cope with their grief.

They got out of the car, the six of them standing together, close. Julie peered into the crowd, hoping to find Aleksander and Bella or someone else she knew. But all were strangers, except that they shared a certain haunted look, and she wondered whether others saw that look in her eyes, too.

"They're not here," Julie said. "Let's leave. This is terrible."

"We have to stay," Niels said. "The soldiers could be watching us."

The sudden sounds of an organ split the air, heavy and commanding. Everyone froze, silent: it might have been a voice from heaven, so immediate and complete was the change. People filed into the church now, orderly and solemn, as if the sham were reality; someone had died and they were going quietly to pay their respects.

They sat with all the others though the mock funeral while the priest, speaking in a low and urgent tones, repeatedly assured everyone that they would be well hidden until passage to Sweden could be arranged.

"Is there space for us all in the church?" one man called out excitedly.

The crowd began to murmur and stir. The priest said, "Yes, we have more room in the loft above us. Do not worry. You will all be safe."

At last the doors were flung open, and Julie made her way with the others back to the car. Along the way Sammy, bewildered by all this strangeness, began to cry and beat at Julie's arm with his fists. "I want Mor," he cried. "Where are we? Where are you taking me?"

"Sammy, Sammy, please calm down."

"I want Mor!" he screamed.

"Sammy, stop hitting me. What's wrong with you?"

"Maybe the medication," Niels said. "It upset him."

"Please, Sammy, be good," Julie pleaded. "Look, I'll buy you orangeade. You'd like that, wouldn't you?" Then she realized that she was penniless. Why hadn't they thought to bring money? Feelings of despair jabbed through her. Wild thoughts raced in her mind. What if she and Sammy were never reunited with her parents? What if they were caught, somehow, trying to get to the coast? How could she manage? And even if there were people to help her, how could she endure being dependent on strangers?

Back in the car, Sammy put his head on Julie's lap. Gently she stroked his hair.

Niels drove them down to the hotel, where Aleksander was supposed to meet them. It was a large, grand old building with a wide porch looking out to sea. Here families came for the summer with countless trunks and nannies for the children. Now a few lone beachcombers poked into the dunes and stared out to sea, where, across the sound, the faint outline of Swedish buildings seemed to float in and out of the mist.

Niels stopped the car. "I'll go and see," he said, getting out.

"I'm going with you," Julie said firmly. "It is my family," she added, realizing how much she sounded like her mother.

Niels sighed. "All right. We'll inquire."

They went first to the pub. Niels reached into his pocket and brought out several kroner. "Would you like something?"

"No, thank you," Julie said. Her eyes stung. It was better to give, she thought, than to receive.

"Six orangeades," Niels said, handing the barkeep several bills. "I'm sure everyone's thirsty."

"Thank you," Julie whispered. They brought the drinks back to the car, then returned to the front of the hotel. As they neared the steps, a figure appeared from the depths of tall shrubs, a man clad all in leather with a cap pulled half over his face.

"Aleksander!" Julie gasped. "Is it you?"

"Oh, Julie, Julie!" Aleksander cried, wringing his hands. "She is not here. They are gone. Oh, my God, what shall I do?"

Niels stepped over to Aleksander. "Where's Aage?"

"He left me off and went back to Copenhagen. There are

others—oh, so many others who need transportation. I told him to go ahead. I thought, of course, that Bella and Sasha would be here! The clerk said they were here, two nights ago. But then the Gestapo came knocking, and Bella and Sasha ran out the back into the forest. They will freeze out there. Bella is not used to such conditions, and my little Sasha, poor Sasha!"

Aleksander's face looked red and chapped where once the beard had been. He clasped Niels's arms, pulling him. "Come! We'll go to the forest. We have to find them. Quickly, we have to go!"

"Look, Aleksander," said Niels, his voice low and patient, "we will help you. Later my uncle Jens is coming. He can get others to organize a search party. But for you to go out alone—there will be patrols, probably with dogs."

"Dogs! Oh, my God, Bella will be terrified!"

"No," Julie said firmly. "Not Bella. She is a brave woman, Aleksander. After all, she decided to come to the coast alone with Sasha. She was wise to leave the hotel. She probably brought blankets and food along, if I know Bella. Later we will go and search, and we will find them." Beneath her bold words Julie felt a terrible nagging apprehension. Bella was hardly the sort of woman to manage an escape.

"Come to my grandfather's house," Niels said quickly, taking Aleksander by the arm. "He will be glad to welcome you."

All the strength seemed to have gone out of Aleksander as he allowed himself to be led to the car, to squeeze in beside Fredericka in front, with barely a glance at anyone, so lost was he in grief. After a few minutes he spoke, turning to Emil. "Does your grandfather have room for all of us?"

Emil said, "Of course. Niels and I can sleep in the barn," he added. "And your boy, too, if he wants."

"Sasha would love that," Aleksander said. Julie heard the tears in his voice.

They drove along the bumpy dirt road behind the dunes, and Julie looked through the waving grasses at the sea, the churning dark gray water sending up spume and mist. At night, without lights or any guidance, how could ships navigate? Julie took a deep breath, determined to keep her mind clear and in the present. Sammy, beside her, strained to look. She pulled him onto her lap and pointed. "Look, Sammy—maybe we can go sailing soon."

He turned and eyed her suspiciously. "I want Mor and Far. Where are they?"

"Oh, they'll be along soon," she said, making her voice bright. "They get to ride in an ambulance, maybe even with the siren on! They will tell us all about it."

The car stopped in front of a white frame house, its paint peeling and porch tilting to one side. The windows were streaked from the salt air, but beneath them were bright blue window boxes filled with dark foliage and plump white blossoms.

Grandfather came out, his arms spread wide, smiling a welcome. "Niels, Emil! Come, come in—ah, the little boy is sleepy. Well, he can curl up in front of the fire. I have everything cozy."

Niels introduced them all. Grandfather took Julie's hand, smiling brilliantly. He had a large, round face, creased from wind and weather and from smiling. His hair was white, his eyes a dazzling blue. "I was expecting a party. Where are your dear parents?"

"They are coming soon," Niels said. "My father is arranging for someone to bring them in an ambulance."

Emil took his grandfather's arm, encircled his back in a swift embrace. "Grandfather! This is Julie's uncle, Aleksander. Later we are going to look for his wife and son. Aleksander came up here on a motorbike."

The old man laughed. "Someday we must get you onto one. In the meantime, tell me what to get for the people. What do you eat, Julie?"

"Why, anything at all, sir. Except—well." She moistened her lips. "We don't eat pork, of course, or—actually, Aleksander is very strict. The best thing would be eggs and potatoes or noodles."

Aleksander nodded and murmured, "Please don't trouble yourself."

"That's all?" exclaimed the grandfather, astonished. "No coffee, tea, fruit, vegetables, or bread?"

"Yes, oh yes, we can eat all of these. Please, don't go to any trouble. I'm sure everything—"

"My dear, I am honored that you are here. It is an insult to feed a person that which he cannot eat. Every faith has its rules, isn't it so? Eggs, we have plenty, praise be to my hens! And corn and peas and beans from the garden. I have rows of canning, did it myself. I will show you."

Emil took Sammy's hand. "Want to see the barn? There is a haystack, maybe some mice in it. Want to see?"

"Go ahead," Julie said with a grateful nod. The two ran out, and Julie sank down on the sofa, Ingrid beside her.

"Fredericka and I are going to take the train back to Copenhagen," Ingrid said softly. "Maybe we can accompany other Jews on the train. They may need help."

Julie nodded. "I'm sure they will." She reached into her pocket for her house key. "Take this, Ingrid," she said. "We might be gone for a long time. There is food in the cooler. My mother and I made soup and special—" Her voice broke. She swallowed, hard, regaining control. "My mother wouldn't want it to go to waste. Take the food. Look in the pantry, too."

"All right, Julie. I will. And I will water the violets in the kitchen."

Julie nodded. "That's good. Once a week is enough. It was Sammy's job."

"I won't forget."

"In my room on the desk are some magazines, almost new."

"I'll save them for you, Julie," Ingrid said.

"No! I want you to have them." Tears spilled down Julie's cheeks. She brushed them aside. "Take them. I want you to."

Ingrid leaned closer, and she drew her arms gently around Julie. "Thank you, Julie."

"For what?" Julie gave a little laugh. "A bunch of old magazines?" She saw Fredericka in the doorway, ready to leave.

Ingrid smiled. "You said they are practically new."

Julie gave her a slight push. "Go. Fredericka is waiting for you. Go and save the world!"

"Write to me, Julie!" Ingrid called.

"Promise to write back!"

"I promise."

"Good-bye, Fredericka—good-bye!"

Grandfather gave them a list of names. "Friends of mine," he said. "They will want to help. You girls can raise money, I'm sure of it, with your pretty smiles! Good-bye, take care. Godspeed!"

Then they were gone. And it seemed to Julie that *good-bye* was the loneliest word in the language. It lingered in the room, an echo of her good-bye to her parents just three days ago. Was it only three days? Incredible. She thought suddenly of Helga, incarcerated these many, many months, and all the others who lived from day to day, prayer to prayer. How did they endure all those good-byes?

Sammy and Emil came running in. Sammy was restored, leaping and shouting, red-cheeked. "Julie! There's little mice in the hay and dogs all over—big dogs, you can run with them on the beach. Emil took me to the shore. Look! I found all these shells, hundred of them, all sorts and colors."

He opened his hand and the glistening little shells dropped into Julie's cupped palms. "Thank you, Sammy," she said. "These are beautiful. Come on, now, let's help Grandfather with lunch. Afterward, we'll play gin rummy. I'm sure we'll find a pack of cards."

◆ ◆ ◆

Late that afternoon, Niels telephoned home. Then he handed the telephone to Julie. Dr. Nelson told her guardedly, "The shipment is delayed, but don't worry. We will get the medicine to you in plenty of time."

"Doctor!" she cried in alarm. "Is the shipment—lost?"

"No, no, not lost," he replied. "Only slightly damaged."

"I understand." Questions circled unceasingly in Julie's mind. Where were they? Was her mother well enough to travel? What about that hacking cough she often heard in the night, and Mother's footsteps as she made her way to the kitchen for a cup of hot tea with honey? A few weeks ago Julie had gotten up and found her mother sitting at the kitchen table, drawing lines and circles on a scrap of paper.

Suddenly she had said, "Julie, do you remember the story of Lot's wife?"

"Why are you teaching me Bible in the middle of the night?" Julie exclaimed.

"Why not?" Her mother brushed her aside. "Lot's wife looked back and turned into pillar of salt. Remember?"

"Of course I remember."

"There is a lesson in that story, Julie. We must never look back. Only move on."

Near nightfall Jens came rushing in. Julie and Niels intercepted him at the door. "Where are Julie's parents?" Niels asked. "Have you heard anything?"

"Dr. Nelson said they'd be here this afternoon," Julie said. "What could have happened?"

"I'm sorry, I don't know anything. Copenhagen is under siege—Gestapo everywhere. But I'm sure Karl will keep your parents safe. The important thing is to start getting people across. We have gotten several boats out of Copenhagen harbors, but we have to keep moving, or the Nazis will suspect. So we are moving up the coast to different harbors. We will find the right place for you and your family."

"But I thought Emil was taking us in his grandfather's boat," said Julie.

"How can you imagine such a thing?" Grandfather exclaimed, throwing up his hands in horror. "First of all, the harbor is mined, and you do not know where. Only the commercial fishermen know this. Secondly, the engine is at its last gasp. What if it were to die in the middle of the sea? You would all be forsaken, probably picked up by a German patrol, if you didn't drown first."

"But I have no money for passage," cried Julie. "No money at all."

Jens shook his head and said soberly, "Nobody will be left behind for lack of money."

He paused, glancing at Sammy, who was cutting pictures out of a magazine, then he drew her aside. "I have to ask you something, Julie," he said seriously. "If I can get passage for you and Sammy, will you go?"

"What do you mean? Just take Sammy and—what about my parents? My relatives? You mean I should just leave everybody?" The idea filled her with alarm. "No! Please, don't ask me to do this, Jens. I could never—"

"I just thought it is something you should be thinking about," he said. "Look, I must go now. There are so many things to do."

"Can't I do something?"

"Yes, indeed. You keep your little brother amused, and keep yourself calm."

◆ ◆ ◆

The men stood ready to go. Julie pulled on her jacket and wrapped her muffler over her head. "I'm ready."

"Julie. We don't need you. Stay here with Sammy," Niels said.

Aleksander stomped about, smacking his hands together, his eyes wild with eagerness to leave.

"I'm coming with you," Julie said firmly. "With four of us, we can split up, two and two. Neither you nor Emil knows Bella and Sasha. So you do need me."

"Why?" Niels demanded. "Why do you insist, Julie?"

"I don't know," she said miserably, though it did seem that she had to prove something to herself, maybe to God, so He would answer her prayer and spare Mother and bring them all together again.

Niels looked aggravated. "All right. But don't complain if you are cold."

"I won't." She met his look, unflinching.

Outside, the darkness enveloped them. From a distance they could hear the baying of dogs, the rumble of patrol boats flashing an occasional beam of light, searching for saboteurs, for rescuers, for runaway Jews.

They drove for a time in silence, without headlights, pushing through heavy mist. At last they stopped at the edge of the forest and left the car under a cover of thick brush.

Julie felt the icy dampness against her face and her hands. She longed for gloves. Woolen stockings. *Selfish creature!* she chided herself, realizing that Bella and Sasha had been out for two days and nights, likely starving, while she had a warm coat and full stomach and the protection of Niels, who grasped her hand. Dogs bayed at a distance. A patrol? Her stomach lurched.

"We'll go left," Niels said to Emil and Aleksander. "If you spot them, whistle, like this." He cupped his hand to his mouth and whistled high and low, high and low. "Let's meet back at the car in two hours." Then he took Julie's hand and pulled her along beside him into the damp darkness of the trees.

Time seemed distorted, direction tangled. "Do you know these trails?" Julie gasped.

"Yes," Niels answered. "Hush!" He beamed his small flashlight into the trees, down onto the ground, into shrubs. "Danes!" he called softly. "We are Danes!"

Motion and pain were the only thoughts in Julie's mind as she ran, stumbled, fell, and rose up again. Pebbles lodged in her socks. Icy cold water soaked her feet. Branches slapped at her face, cut into her hands. Her breath felt frozen inside her chest, and she gasped out, calling in harsh whispers, "Bella! Sasha!" Now and again they came upon a form or forms huddled together, faces raised, white, alarmed. Then Niels told them, "Make your way to the church in Gilleleje—out of the forest here, due south. They will take you in! Go!"

And Julie implored them, "Have you seen a woman with a boy, twelve years old? The boy's name is Sasha."

"Many—we have seen many people. Do you have food? Something to drink?"

"We'll send help," Niels said, and Julie looked up at him in wonder that he could keep his head while she felt distracted and torn to pieces. "Some scouting groups are searching. They will bring you out. Go to the edge. You will see."

After a time Julie's feet and lips felt numb.

"Are you all right?" Niels asked. "Your hand is so cold." He rubbed her hands in his as they hurried along. "We've been out two hours. Time to go back and meet Emil and Aleksander. Maybe they—"

They heard the whistle, twice, three times.

Found! *Oh, God,* Julie prayed, *let them be safe.*

Chapter Thirty-two

Niels

All the time he was dragging her beside him, Niels felt his mind raging on opposing themes. Why did she have to come along? Stubborn and difficult, why couldn't she stay home and let him take care of things? Then he felt her hand in his, became aware of her halting breath, saw how she stumbled and fell and rose up again without complaint, and he wanted to say something encouraging, to tell her how brave she was, how good.

By the time they found Emil and Aleksander at the car, Julie's hair was dripping wet, and when she saw Bella in Aleksander's arms, lying limp, her head and arms hanging down, Niels though she would scream out loud. But Julie sprang into action. She ran to the car and flung open the doors, shouting, "Sasha! Get into the car. Quick! Aleksander, lay her down on the backseat." She pulled off her parka and spread it over the unconscious woman. "Go! We have to get her to the house."

Suddenly it was Julie taking charge while he and the others could only stare dumbly during Sasha's fearful recitation. "We left so fast—I grabbed a blanket—we were freezing and hungry. I dug into some leaves. Then Mama said—we had to take—the poison. Because they would catch us. And torture us. She gave me a pill. She swallowed one. But I dropped mine. Is she dead? Is she dead?"

Aleksander and Julie crouched in the back as Niels went speeding along the narrow roadway. He had turned on the headlights now, and they sliced through the dense fog, sending back a misty white glare. Suddenly a siren sounded, and a bright beam cut through the haze.

"Do you have it?" Emil murmured.

"Yes." Emil had returned the pistol to Niels when they got to his grandfather's house. He felt the butt against waist.

A motorcycle roared up beside the car. Light blazed into Niels's eyes. *"Austeigen!"*

Niels turned toward the back, where Aleksander knelt beside his wife, rubbing her hands.

"We have a sick woman here," Niels said loudly. "We are taking her to hospital."

Only one guard, he thought—a loner. In a moment he could draw out the pistol, push open the door, take aim, shoot. In a flash he rehearsed it, each movement smooth, flowing to the next—draw, push, aim, *shoot.*

He said, "We have to hurry. It is a matter of life and death! Come, be human . . ." Niels reached for the pistol, drew it out, and held it close to his thigh. His other hand grasped the door handle, pulled up.

The soldier shone his flashlight into the backseat. He stood stock-still for a moment. A small cross around his neck gleamed brightly. "Ah," he said. "Joseph and Mary, I see—Jews. Go on! Get out of here!"

Niels's heart thumped in his chest, his mind fragmented on

the amazing circumstance, the cross, his plea for humanity—or was it sheer luck? How slight, he thought, how very narrow the margin between life and death.

The tires made a bleating sound on the wet pavement as Niels gunned the motor and sped away into the night. He opened the window to let the cold wind strike his face, for no other reason than to realize that he was fully alive, and had not killed a man.

"I think she is breathing," came Julie's voice from the back. "Hurry! We have to make her vomit! Hurry!"

Niels ran ahead, kicked upon the door. Aleksander and Emil carried Bella into the house. Julie ran to the small kitchen, calling for Grandfather. "Salt and water and mustard—hurry! She ate poison."

"How do you know, Julie? How do you know?" Aleksander entreated, beating his chest. "What if you are wrong? What if she dies?"

"Niels! Call the hospital," Julie ordered. "Hurry! Ask them . . ."

He ran to the telephone. His hands trembled as he dialed. "Emergency!" he shouted into the receiver. A fire blazed in the hearth. Sweat poured into his eyes. Julie stood beside him, the cup shaking in her hands.

A woman on the other end of the line said, "Salt water and mustard—or soap. Get it down her, as much as you can."

He turned to Julie with a nod. "You are right. Hurry!"

It was a nightmare of forced feeding, retching, feeding, fighting, rejecting. At last Bella opened her eyes. She began to tremble violently. Grandfather burst into tears. "Praise God! Thank you, Jesus!"

Later, when Bella lay resting before the fire on a quilt, Sasha and Aleksander beside her, Niels went to Julie. She stood in the kitchen, leaning against the table, immobile. A strange thought came to him, a fantasy, that he was the surgeon and Julie his assistant.

"Julie, how did you know what to do?" he asked.

She shook her head. "Maybe I read it somewhere. Maybe I heard about it from someone. I don't know," she said. "It just flew into my mind. Maybe a miracle." She laughed slightly. "Not that I believe much in miracles."

"You are a miracle," he found himself saying. He reached for her hands. Gently he drew her to him. She lifted her face. His lips found hers. First cold, then warm, her lips were indescribably soft and sweet, and he felt a great tenderness and longing. *Oh, if only, if only we . . . why now? Why so late?* "Julie," he whispered. "Julie."

A sharp blast of air was hurled into the kitchen, accompanied by a thump and a hearty shout. "Oh! Niels!" Jens strode in, slamming the back door behind him, dressed as he had been that night at the lake, his cheeks blackened, a dark knitted cap pulled over his ears. "Listen, I think I've got a boat. We have to go immediately. Julie, there is space for twelve people. I have two families already, nine people altogether. I can take you and Sammy, and one more."

Aleksander stood in the doorway. "Take Sasha," he said. "Julie, you can take Sasha to Sweden."

"No! No, Aleksander." She backed toward the wall. "You three go. I'll stay here and wait for my parents."

"Bella can't go tonight. She is barely conscious. You go, Julie, please, I beg you. Take the boys. We will meet you in Sweden. Julie, if we have a chance to save our child—don't take this away from us."

Niels saw how she closed her eyes, trying to blot out the inevitable. He saw her draw a deep breath, steeling herself.

"All right. We'll go."

"How do we get to the harbor?" Niels asked.

"I'll take them," Jens said. "We have to walk. Cars are suspect."

"I'm going, too," Niels declared.

Jens hesitated. "All right. We have to keep down. We are meeting at the fisherman's house."

Julie buttoned Sammy into his jacket and added a dark woolen shawl from Grandfather, which she wound around his head and shoulders. "Keep your hands in your pockets," she ordered. "And don't say a word. No matter what happens, don't say a word!"

"Are we going to a new home?"

"Yes."

"Are we orphans, then?"

"No! Never say that again!"

"Your parents will follow," Niels told Sammy.

"Promise?"

"I promise. If I have to bring them myself in a rowboat." He was speaking to Sammy but looking at Julie. Niels saw her struggle, realizing how, in these last few days, he had come to know her so well. He knew her fear of being left alone in a strange land, having to take care of Sammy, grieving for her parents.

"I'm coming, too," said Emil, pulling on his jacket. "I'll carry Sammy on my back. We can take turns."

Jens hesitated, then nodded. "All right. Let's go. Sasha! Come on!"

Aleksander and Sasha stood in the corner speaking softly. Niels averted his eyes. It seemed wrong to watch, wrong to be part of this moment, even as a bystander. He heard Aleksander murmur some strange, foreign-sounding words, saw an object pass from father to son. Sasha pushed something into the front of his jacket, then he buttoned up, keeping his arms close around himself.

Jens prodded them, "Come on. It will take nearly an hour to get there. We don't have all night!"

Once again they were accosted by the biting cold, the wind, the dampness. They trudged along the road without speaking. Niels held Julie's hand. He and Emil took turns carrying Sammy on their backs. With Julie's hand in his, it seemed impossible that he was taking her to the harbor, and that she would leave. All he wanted was to keep on walking, holding her hand.

The roads were empty, save for an occasional passerby or a truck. Headlights blinded them for a moment and quickly faded away. They kept to the edge of the road, where the heavy fog settled over them, and the limbs of trees swirled and the wind blew in piercing gusts.

At last they turned into a narrow lane to a small house with a thatch roof, its thick whitewashed walls and window boxes looking serene in the moonlight that now showed faintly through the clouds. Jens rapped loudly at the door. It was immediately flung open, and the young fisherman, bearded and wild eyed, urged them to enter. "Quick! Get in. Shut the door! Look, I cannot do this. The harbor is mined. My friends tell me there is a Nazi patrol twice every night . . ."

Jens reached into his pocket, thumped down a handful of bills on the scarred wooden table. "You promised," he said.

"I did not realize the danger!" the fisherman cried. He was short but stocky. Thick muscles showed through his shirt. His hands, outspread, were coarse and tough from weather and wear.

"Look, if they catch me, they will sink my boat. Or worse. I have a family, a wife and two little girls . . ."

In that moment his wife appeared. "The girls are sleeping," she said softly. She moved to her husband's side, slid her hand into his. "I have been thinking, Torben. If you do not take them, what will we tell our girls later, when they ask us what we did?"

He looked down at her, his expression perplexed. "What are you saying, Anne?"

"That if we do not help them," she replied, "we are as bad as the Nazis. We allow them to do what they will."

The fisherman stared at his wife, then at Jens. "Wait," he said. He pulled his wife to a place under the window, where Niels could see them in silhouette, talking and gesturing. At one point the man put his hand on his wife's hair. Her voice was gentle but entreating, only a murmur.

At last the fisherman came back to Jens. "Very well," he said. "I will take them. But I warn you, I do not know the Swedish waters very well. I am only a stone fisherman, and I do not sail out to the limits."

"You need only take them to the island," said Jens. "There, a Swedish fishing boat will meet them."

"You can do it, Torben," said his wife, beaming.

The fisherman turned and strode to the cabinet where dishes were kept, and he reached deep inside and brought out a bottle of amber liquid. "It gets very cold out on the water," he said.

"Then let's all take a good drink," said his wife, "for warmth." She turned to Niels and Julie and Emil with a broad smile. "You all look as if you could use a sip," she added, filling six small glasses to the brim.

Niels handed one to Julie. "To your health," he murmured.

"L'chaim," she said, tasting the brandy with the tip of her tongue.

"To life," he repeated. "You see, I know the word."

"I was sure you did," she said.

They went down to the dock, where boats pitched in the water, restless and lurching in the swells. Never had Niels felt so helpless and at the same time so certain that what he did at this moment mattered more than any other action in his life.

Jens told Julie, "You will have to get down in the hold, where they carry the boulders. It will be dark, but he will leave it open a crack so you will have air."

Others were gathering, dark shapes, their hands pressed to their faces, fearful, stunned by what they were about to do. The men climbed down first, held out their hands to the women. A baby was handed down, squirming, making squeaking sounds, like a cat. Quickly the sounds were silenced, somehow. It seemed incredible that so many people could fit into that space, or that they could remain there in the dank darkness, pressed together, with scarcely room to breathe.

"Sasha, go down," Julie said.

Sasha opened his mouth to speak, then nodded and looked up to the sky before he lowered his head and stepped down.

"Sammy—don't say a word."

Sammy nodded.

"You go to Sasha. He and I will hold on to you every moment, do you understand?"

"Yes," Sammy whispered.

"Good-bye, Niels," Julie whispered. Then she stepped down into the darkness.

Niels watched as the fisherman closed the cover over the hold. Now there was only the empty, dark deck, the large, powerful winch that the fisherman used to bring up boulders from the bottom of the sea, and several nets flung about.

"Let me go with you!" Niels suddenly cried. "I can help you. I can do whatever you say!"

The fisherman turned and looked at him, a strange, crooked smile on his lips. "You? Show me your hands!"

Niels held out his hands. A lantern on the dock cast a meager light.

"Ha! Those are the hands of a student. Nobody in his right mind would take you for a sailor! Go on. I will do this alone. You can bring me more cargo. Might as well keep going once I've figured out the way!"

Emil stepped forward. "I will go with you," he declared. "I know all the coves and islands. My grandfather and I have sailed to Sweden dozens of times."

Niels glanced at Jen questioningly. Jens nodded and shrugged.

"Emil!" Niels called, grasping Emil's arm. "You don't have to do this."

"Yes, I do," Emil said, his lips firm. "It is exactly what I have to do."

The stone fisherman gave Emil a long, appraising look. At last he clapped Emil on the back. "Come along, then."

Emil stepped aboard, and his body immediately found balance against the swaying of the boat. His stance told more than words: this was what he was born for.

As the boat pulled away, Niels heard the skipper telling Emil, "Now heave in the anchor. Steady there. Keep your eyes peeled . . ."

Niels and Jen stood watching the small craft recede into the mist. Niels heard the soft purr of the motor, saw the ripples in the water, felt the chill in his bones and the pitching dock beneath his feet. He could imagine the terrifying darkness inside the hold of that boat. Then he made himself think of the dawn, how Julie and the others would come out of that darkness into light and safety.

Niels felt as if a song were rising to his lips. He felt an explosive gladness beyond words.

"Well done," said Jens, and together he and Niels made their way back to the house.

Chapter Thirty-three

Julie

When the lid came down, and darkness was complete, Julie felt a leaping in her chest, bands across her throat, panic. Panic threatened to burst from her mouth, her nose, her pores. She felt crammed, buried alive. The terrible darkness! Like death.

Had it not been for Sammy and Sasha, she would have lost all reason. She would have screamed out, even forsaking the chance of rescue just to breathe the night air again, not to be stuffed into this hole, where strangers pressed against her and the darkness had substance, like a heavy bag over her head.

In that deadly silence, eventually sounds came clear: the lapping of the water, the soft creaking of boards, the distant clink of a chain. Julie stood motionless, listening now to the faint sounds of breathing and stirring, sounds of rubbing fibers, wood, hair. Things seemed to crawl along her arms and down her back, into every fissure of her body. The darkness itself held eerie specks, not of light, but of deep color. Fragments seemed to break off and dart before her line of vision. She felt the sweat on her hand, where Sasha held on to her, and the tension in her fingers around Sammy's arm.

The boat heaved. Sour curdling tastes rose to Julie's mouth.

She swallowed them down again and again. Something deep in her stomach seemed to yawn widely, then to constrict. Visions of snakes danced before her eyes, visions of fire and bones.

Julie forced herself to breathe deep, making a rhythm, and she made herself think the words *calm, calm. Peace. Love.* And she collected her thoughts, forced them into a question. How does one overcome this darkness? How?

Answers flooded into her mind, as if she had only to ask the question. *Music,* said her mind, *Think music. Love,* said her mind, *Think love. Think of music and people you love.*

There was a world of memories to replay, pieces of music to recite in her mind. She could blot out the present by replacing it with the eternal—with music and memories. She breathed now in quiet rhythm of Chopin, the waltzes, the preludes, the "Polonaise." And when the music was finished, she took out her memories—mornings in the snow, when the crystals sparkled in the sunshine and the drifts were packed with pale blue and purple shadows. Evenings when the sun poured down gold and crimson, and clouds rode at the edge of the sea like phantom ships. The smell of lilies, the warmth of candle wax, the taste of roasted meat and savory potatoes, the creamy chocolate on her tongue, the taste of raspberries, different from strawberries and blueberries, and after that she remembered all the tastes of fruits and marveled at the richness of life. The most amazing, most personal memory she saved for last. She saw herself again in the kitchen with Niels, and now she replayed every second of that brief encounter—the way he walked, the way he looked at her, his hands touching hers, the sound of his voice, the nearness of his face, his lips on hers—his lips on hers.

A shout from above erased the vision. Everyone tensed; bones seemed to lock into place, and the air was foul with the smell of fear. Not even a moan or a sigh sounded, only the shouts and the footsteps above Julie's head, like nails being driven into her skull, and the white-hot terror from behind her eyes shrieking, shrieking, *Let me out!*

The voices expanded, filled the dark space completely. Other sounds drifted down, something being opened, banged shut, more voices, laughter, and then they receded into nothing but the humming sounds of the motor and water lapping against the boat.

Julie felt the first whiff of air as the lid was raised. The night air seeped down into the hold, and the fisherman called down joyously, "You can come up now! They are gone. I gave them a good deal of fresh fish to keep them busy. Those Germans—always hungry, they'll sell their soul for a herring and their heart for a beer!"

The fisherman was changed and charmed, jovial and strong, as if he owned the sea and everything in it, as if he were Neptune. Emil, too, had come alive, joking with the fisherman, his blond hair wet from the ocean spray.

Julie stood with the other passengers on the deck, lined along the edges, as if their searching could hasten the voyage and bring them to land. They drifted, surged forward, changed course. The fisherman alternately checked his charts, cursed, called out a passionate, "Aha! Now!" And soon the darkness reached its peak, that epitome of darkness before dawn, periwinkle color beginning at the edges, like a giant cloth unfolding, adding a wash of lavender and gray. Julie, watching the sky parade its colors, thought of Ingrid and how she would lavish paints onto paper and yet never approach the perfection of this true miracle. It is only the sky, she told herself. The sky.

◆ ◆ ◆

Julie sat at the small wooden table that Far had placed in front of the window so that she could see the shores of Denmark whenever she looked up from her schoolwork. She dipped her pen into the ink and began, having composed this letter in her mind for the past three weeks:

Dear Ingrid, Fredericka, and Niels,

Please forgive this long delay, but we have been incredibly busy since our arrival. We had to find a home, enroll in school, and make all sorts of contacts. The agency has found a job for Far in an antiques store! They also sell estate jewelry. He is thrilled. They never had an expert in canes before, so the feeling is mutual. Mother was very weak when she arrived here; they had to carry her out on a stretcher. Now she continues to improve, thanks to a wonderful team of doctors. She is able to walk to the harbor with me every afternoon. Sammy is in first grade and already learning some Swedish words.

Julie paused, wondering how much detail to give them about that awful journey. She decided to dwell, instead, on the rescue.

I'm not sure how long we were under way. It seemed like forever! At last the captain shouted, "We are here! I have found it! The island—I see the Swedish boat, the skipper is waving."

You can imagine our joy at being on Swedish soil, seeing the boat with the Swedish flag coming toward us, the sailors shouting, "Welcome! Welcome to Sweden!"

We assembled there on that barren island, and as we waited for the Swedish boat to land, Sasha took the shofar out of his jacket, where he had held it the whole night through. We all faced east, toward Jerusalem, and we prayed the Jewish prayer of thanksgiving. Oh, our voices were strong! Then Sasha blew that ram's horn loud—so loud! I felt chills moving down my spine at the sound of it. I have never heard it blown so loudly, so well. There were tears on Sasha's face. Two days later, when Sasha's parents arrived, they heard about it, and they were so proud of their son.

We were taken to a relocation center and given a room in a dormitory along with many other people. I tried to telephone you, but could not get through. The woman at the agency told me you would be notified. Did they tell you of our safe arrival? Thanks to you, my parents joined us the very next day. How did you manage it? They say that nearly all the Jews escaped, helped by friends and even by strangers.

I am at school now with many other Danish students, finishing my last year, preparing for university. We hear that the German army is growing weaker after defeats in Africa and Italy. I know the day will come when we can return home. At this moment I am sitting by the window looking out to sea, at Denmark. It is a lovely land.

Until we meet again,
Yours,
Julie

Chapter Thirty-Four

Willi

Liebe Mutti,

I have not much time to write, for Dr. Best keeps me busy preparing statements and filing papers. He uses me continually for all manner of important work, trusting few others.

Soon you will be hearing rumors of events in Denmark. I must admonish you, with all due respect: do not believe everything you hear. Much of it is only propaganda by the Allies, who refuse to admit that they will soon be defeated, and that they will have to serve a new master.

Suffice it to say that our goal has been achieved: Denmark is now free of Jews. Soon the entire world will acknowledge our victory! However small a part I have played in this, I hope I have made you proud of

Your faithful son,
Willi

Chapter Thirty-five

Fredericka's Diary

I have been so busy working that there has been no time to reflect or to write. Ingrid and I went door to door and raised an amazing amount of money to pay sailors and fishermen for the risks they took to ferry the Jews to Sweden. We traveled by train and car, taking people to the north. We gathered blankets and food. For a few weeks, every waking moment was devoted to this, and I must say, it was one of the best times of my life.

After Julie and her family left, we all felt such great joy and accomplishment. We showed the Germans, at last, who is who in Denmark, and that they cannot dominate us. It was a wonderful, unbelievable victory to watch those ships setting out, knowing we were sending all those people to freedom.

Of course, not everyone was saved, but someone told me that over seven thousand Jews escaped. Only a few hundred were caught. Among them was Julie's grandmother Sophie. They sent her to Theresienstadt. That dignified, proud woman! She simply refused to eat, and after ten days she died.

Happier news came from Julie's other relatives, Boris, and his son, Michael. Apparently they had made their way to Hornbaek on the train, then to the church at Gilleleje, where so many of the

Jews were hidden. A maid who worked at the hotel informed the Gestapo that Jews were hidden in the church loft. Because of her, eighty people were arrested and taken away to concentration camps. Boris was trying to take matters into his own hands, and had gone to negotiate passage with some sailors. His son had run after him. So when the Nazis came to the church loft, they didn't get those two. What luck! Why are some saved and others doomed?

Maybe it is for the novelist to figure out such things.

I am starting to work on a novel about the resistance and rescue. There are hundreds, thousands of heroic stories. I want to focus not on the evil, but on the goodness that exists in this world. That is not to say I will ever forget or forgive what they did to us. Every day I think of Peter. Is he still alive? Will I ever see him again? But I don't dwell on that hope, or on despair. We must move on. Life is so precious, it must be lived fully and with joy.

AUTHOR'S NOTE

The events in this story reflect a basic truth: of all the lands that Hitler conquered, and of all the tyranny he and his armies imposed, in Denmark he could not rule. The people of Denmark, steeped in democratic tradition and goodwill, simply would not permit their Jewish friends, neighbors, and coworkers to be singled out for oppression and persecution. Thus, of the country's nearly eight thousand Jews, only several hundred were captured, arrested, and sent to concentration camps. Even while they were incarcerated, the Danish people, together with the Red Cross, kept up an incessant clamor for their safety. After the war, most Danish Jews returned to their homes. They were greeted with the same kindness and respect that had marked their hasty departure.

All the events in this story are based on true experiences that were related to me, either in documents and books or personal interviews, by rescuers and survivors of this gallant episode in history. For the sake of the novel, I have created composite characters and situations to reflect both the heroism and the disgrace, the good and the bad in human nature.

The Danish resistance and rescue stand as evidence that man

can rise to the challenges of his time and achieve greatness of spirit even in the face of evil.

I offer my profound thanks to the people of Denmark and to their descendants for their remarkable courage, which remains a standard for all humanity.

Bibliography

Bamberger, Ib Nathan. *The Viking Jews: A History of the Jews of Denmark.* New York: Socino Press, 1983.

Barfod, Jorgen H. *Denmark 1940–1945: This Happened During Denmark's Fight for Freedom.* Copenhagen: Frihedsmuseets Venner, 1984.

Bertelson, Aage. *October 43,* London: Museum Press, 1955.

Goldberger, Leo, editor. *The Rescue of the Danish Jews: Moral Courage Under Stress.* New York: New York University Press, 1987.

Ipsen, Anne. *A Child's Tapestry of War: Denmark 1940–1945.* Edina, Minn.: Beavers Pond Press, 1998.

Levine, Ellen. *Darkness over Denmark: The Danish Resistance and the Rescue of the Jews.* New York: Holiday House, 2000.

Loeffler, Martha. *Boats in the Night: Knud Dyby's Involvement in the Rescue of the Danish Jews and the Danish Resistance.* Blair, Nebr.: Lur Publications Danish Immigrant Archive, Dan College, 2000.

Pundik, Herbert. *In Denmark It Could Not Happen: The Flight of the Jews to Sweden in 1943.* Jerusalem and New York: Gefen Books, 1998.

Skov, Niels Aage. *Letter to My Descendants.* Odense, Denmark: Odense University Press, 1999.

Sutherland, Christine. *Monica: Heroine of the Danish Resistance.* New York: Farrar, Straus & Giroux, 1990.

Yahill, Leni. *The Rescue of Danish Jewry: Test of a Democracy.* Philadelphia: Jewish Publication Society of America, 1969.